1 0 STEPS TO

Successful Presentations

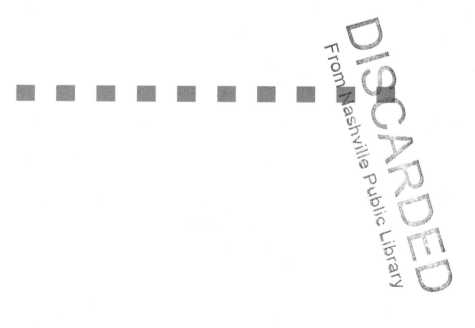

ASTD
WORKPLACE LEARNING & PERFORMANCE
PRESS
Alexandria, Virginia

ASTD Press is an internationally renowned source of insightful and practical information on workplace learning and performance topics, including training basics, evaluation and return on investment, instructional systems development, e-learning, leadership, and career development.

Ordering information: Books published by ASTD Press can be purchased by visiting our website at store.astd.org or by calling 800.628.2783 or 703.683.8100.

Library of Congress Control Number: 2008927846
ISBN-10: 1-56286-514-5
ISBN-13: 978-1-56286-514-6

ASTD Press Editorial Staff:
Director: Cat Russo
Manager, Acquisitions and Author Relations: Mark Morrow
Editorial Manager: Jacqueline Edlund-Braun
Editorial Assistant: Maureen Soyars
Retail Trade Manager: Yelba Quinn

Writer: Lynn S. Lewis
Copyeditor: Pamela Lankas
Indexer: Mary Kidd
Proofreader: International Graphic Services
Interior Design and Production: International Graphic Services
Cover Design: Ana Ilieva

Printed by Victor Graphics, Inc., Baltimore, Maryland, www.victorgraphics.com

10 STEPS TO SUCCESS

Let's face it, most people spend their days in chaotic, fast-paced, time- and resource-strained organizations. Finding time for just one more project, assignment, or even learning opportunity—no matter how career enhancing or useful—is difficult to imagine. The *10 Steps* series is designed for today's busy professional who needs advice and guidance on a wide array of topics ranging from project management to people management, from business strategy to decision making and time management, from stepping in to deliver a presentation for someone else to researching and creating a compelling presentation to effectively deliver the content. Each book in this series promises to take its readers on a journey to basic understanding, with practical application the ultimate destination. This is truly a just-tell-me-what-to-do-now series. You will find action-driven language teamed with examples, worksheets, case studies, and tools to help you quickly implement the right steps and chart a path to your own success. The *10 Steps* series will appeal to a broad business audience from middle managers to upper-level management. Workplace learning and human resource professionals along with other professionals seeking to improve their value proposition in their organizations will find these books a great resource.

C O N T E N T S

P R E F A C E

You have probably attended a presentation at one time or another led by a charismatic presenter who leveraged effective facilitation techniques to draw audience participation and whose enthusiasm about the topic was contagious. Whether the presentation was to provide information or to illicit a call to action, the presenter's skills and structure of the content probably had a great deal of impact on what you remembered and acted on after the presentation.

The thought of giving a presentation often ranks at the top of the list of what people fear the most. So how do you go about developing and delivering an effective, memorable presentation? *10 Steps to Successful Presentations* provides the key information you need to accomplish this goal. You can jump to any step in the 10-step process or start at the beginning. These steps include

1. knowing your audience and purpose
2. developing and structuring the presentation
3. creating appropriate visual aids
4. making it memorable—adding pizzazz to the presentation
5. making sure venue and environment work in your favor
6. reviewing basic communication techniques
7. building in facilitation techniques to engage your audience
8. practicing, practicing, practicing
9. pausing and refreshing
10. delivering a flawless presentation—no matter what happens.

Most of what is presented in this book is based on real-world experience as well as observation of presentations that either wowed the audience or fell short, motivating participants to quickly head for the door.

10 Steps to Successful Presentations is part of ASTD's *10-Step* series and was written to provide you with a proven process, quick reference checklists, and tips to create and deliver an effective presentation. We hope that the tips and tools contained in this book will guide you each step of the way in developing and delivering a presentation.

INTRODUCTION

Standing in the spotlight to effectively communicate information that an audience needs or wants can be a truly scary experience—no matter what your level of experience of presenting in front of an audience. Whether you are a guest speaker presenting on a topic that someone else chose or presenting data to C-level managers, the basics to get you started in structuring and presenting the information are the same.

The business acumen expected of today's business professionals includes effective communication and presentation skills. Without these skills, career goals and aspirations may be hindered. This book, *10 Steps to Successful Presentations*, provides a framework you can use to create an effective presentation in a short timeframe. The tips and examples provided in each chapter will help to guide you through this process whether the presentation is for a large- or small-group setting.

Use the key steps in this book as needed. For example, if you have been asked to give an existing presentation; you can focus on steps 4 through 10. Or, if you have been asked to select and present on a topic in which you are starting with a completely blank slate—perhaps how the marketing strategy is poised to support new product revenue goals—then it might be most appropriate to start with step one and work through all of the steps systematically.

10 Steps to Successful Presentations provides proven techniques and tips for creating and delivering a presentation. In particular, this book will show you how to

◆ conduct an audience analysis
◆ plan the presentation outline and develop the content
◆ select visual aids to support and enhance your message
◆ demonstrate polished presentation skills
◆ plan and manage the presentation-room setup
◆ use facilitation techniques to engage the audience
◆ rehearse and perfect your presentation delivery.

Structure of This Book

10 Steps to Successful Presentations will help you to quickly plan, develop, and deliver a successful, compelling presentation. Each section describes one of the 10 specific steps for accomplishing this goal. Here is an overview:

◆ **Step 1: Know Your Audience and Purpose: The Five Ws and More**—No matter how the opportunity to present landed on your calendar, the first step is always to conduct an audience analysis and to answer the following questions—who, what, where, when, and why—in order to develop the purpose of the presentation.

◆ **Step 2: Develop and Structure your Presentation**—whether you need to create a presentation from scratch or embellish and personalize an existing presentation, all successful presentations have five standard components that you need to address. This step outlines strategies for planning to meet and greet the audience, developing your opening, creating transitions to maintain the presentation flow, building the body content, and closing on a bang.

◆ **Step 3: Create Appropriate Visual Aids**—visual aids enable you to enhance your presentation with both high- and low-tech solutions. Not all visual aids are appropriate in all situations—so it is important to understand the plethora of visual aids available and how to determine which visual is most appropriate for your presentation purpose, audience, and environment. This step provides visual-aid guidelines to enhance your successful presentation and not just decorate it.

- **Step 4: Make It Memorable—Add Pizzazz to a Presentation**—with the key and supporting points of the presentation outlined, this step takes your presentation to the next level by adding elements to excite and engage your audience, including ideas for attention-grabbing openers and icebreakers; storytelling tips; appropriate use of humor; and building the content with text, graphs, tables, statistics, and other good stuff.

- **Step 5: Make Sure the Venue and Environment Work in Your Favor**—creating an environment that is well-suited to the presentation is not only important in keeping the audience from heading for the door, but sends the message that as a credible professional, you took the time to consider and set up the environment. This step describes the list of presentation room setup guidelines and tips.

- **Step 6: Stop—Review Basic Communication Techniques**—although there are many different ways to present, there are certain methods and skills that seem to work best in most situations. This step highlights the presentation styles and techniques of the most successful presenters, including verbal and nonverbal skills.

- **Step 7: Build in Facilitation Techniques to Engage Your Audience**—most presenters are involved at one point or another in facilitating a presentation, meaning they involve the audience in open sharing of thoughts, opinions, and ideas. Becoming a strong facilitator is a required skill for any presenter and consists of part art and part science. This step outlines the basics of facilitating discussions and how you can harness these skills for your presentations.

- **Step 8: Practice, Practice, Practice**—a key rule for any presenter is to know the material. Period. Rehearsing the delivery helps to put the icing on the cake. This step focuses on tips and techniques for rehearsing the presentation, practicing theatrics such as telling a joke or story, anticipating stumper questions, and planning your answers.

◆ **Step 9: Pause and Refresh—Relax You'll Do Fine**—sweaty palms and performance butterflies can plague even the most seasoned presenters, so what techniques do the pros use to combat nervousness and harness that energy and anxiety so they work in your favor? This step provides techniques to reduce performance anxiety and build confidence before stepping on the podium.

◆ **Step 10: Deliver a Flawless Presentation—No Matter What Happens**—even presenters who are professional, prepared, and credible will experience some embarrassing moment during their presentation careers. How they plan for and handle those unexpected and potential disasters is what makes the difference between novices and seasoned professionals. This step focuses on how to create a backup plan to get your presentation back on track no matter what happens.

Review these 10 steps as often as needed to build and perfect your ability to create and deliver successful presentations.

Know Your Audience and Purpose: The Five Ws and More

STEP 1

OVERVIEW

Asking the right questions to identify your purpose

Determining the type of presentation

Preparing your elevator speech

Just as journalists need to know the *five Ws*—who, what, where, when, and why—prior to writing a story, you also need to know these same five Ws when planning to create or deliver a presentation.

Presentations may appear on your to-do list in a variety of ways. For example, perhaps you have been asked to present on a topic that requires you to do some research on the topic you will be presenting. At other times, you may be involuntarily scheduled to deliver a stellar presentation at a conference or to the board of directors. No matter which situation has given rise to the opportunity to present, asking the right questions and planning for the presentation are critical steps to success—and in particular this should always be your first step.

In business, presentations are a way of life and can range from a brief presentation before management to a series of talks that may in fact be a form of training. Effective presenters plan every detail to ensure the success of their presentation. Planning includes understanding the audience—that is, performing some sort of analysis by asking questions and creating an audience profile—identifying the objectives or goals for the presentation, researching the topic, and matching the facilities setup to the presentation requirements.

Asking the Right Questions to Identify Your Purpose

Why should participants want to sit in a warm room, elbow to elbow, on uncomfortable chairs and listen to what you have to say for an hour or more? What's the nature of your message—to inform, inspire, or persuade? What value will the presentation provide to participants by its conclusion? The answer to these questions defines the purpose of the presentation and should shape the content and structure of the presentation to benefit the audience. The "right" questions you need to ask fall into five categories—who, what, where, when, and why. The process involves asking questions to conduct a quick analysis and develop an audience profile to get a sense of who is in the audience (their background education and experience, their gender and cultural mix) and to determine the focus of the presentation.

Who: Conducting an Audience Analysis and Determining the WIIFM

POINTER

Always conduct an audience analysis. It provides invaluable information.

Answering the question of "who" provides you with insight into the target audience for your presentation. In an ideal situation, you have all the information you need about the audience before you begin creating or delivering the presentation. If you don't have this information, and you have time to collect it, then you should invest the time to perform an audience analysis by gathering answers to key "who" questions.

Because no two audiences are alike, you should always conduct an audience analysis even if you are delivering an existing or canned presentation. This step not only helps you to determine the purpose of your presentation but is invaluable in helping you anticipate questions and hot topics and tailoring the content to meet specific audience needs. Consider each presentation as an opportunity to meet new peers, showcase your skills and knowledge, and build credibility. The first key to successful presentations is to know your audience so that you can make the presentation content relevant and valuable to them.

Key Questions to Determine "Who" Is in the Audience:

◆ Are participant positions higher, lower, or even with your position on an organization chart?

◆ Are they affiliated with a particular industry or profession?

◆ Do they hold a shared point of view about the topic or divergent views?

◆ To what degree do you expect them to agree with your point of view?

◆ Are they required to attend the presentation or is it voluntary?

◆ How many of them are there in relation to the size of the room/auditorium?

◆ What do you know about their motives, aspirations, interests, and desires (for example, what are their jobs and leisure activities)?

◆ What is their educational background and knowledge of the topic to be discussed?

◆ What age range is expected?

◆ What is the proportion of men to women?

◆ What are their racial/ethnic heritages?

◆ What geographic areas/regions do they represent?

◆ What is the audience's knowledge or expertise with regard to the topic you are presenting?

◆ Are there any decision-makers in the audience? What are their most important needs?

◆ What objections are likely?

These questions should be directed to the presentation sponsor—the person who asked you to make the presentation. If the sponsor is unavailable to answer these questions, find out who can help you to identify this information. Verify that your sponsor and you are on the same page with regard to what the audience is expected to gain or be expected to do as a result of your speech. Be specific; inquire about the audience's needs and find out if there is specific terminology used by the audience so that you can speak in their terms and build credibility.

POINTER

"Need to know" information in a presentation usually amounts to about three to five points that may be provided by the sponsor, a senior executive, audience members, or subject matter experts who can help you understand what the audience really needs to know when preparing the presentation.

Identifying the WIIFM

Presentation attendees possess various motivations for attending the presentation. You probably won't know all of them prior to stepping on the podium, but anticipating what they might be will help you to effectively prepare, anticipate questions, and structure the presentation. For example, some attendees may attend because they were told to do so and others may willingly attend to increase their knowledge of the subject. Regardless of their motivation for attending you need to consider the WIIFM—what's in it for me—since the participants will be asking themselves this question.

Some presentation participants will be highly motivated to hear something new, get clarification on questions, or have the opportunity to network. As a presenter, keep in mind that these same participants may ask the most challenging questions since they are taking the content and the opportunity to ask questions seriously.

What: Conducting Topic and Content Research

In the event that you are asked to speak on a particular topic, do some research and take time to think about the opportunity before agreeing to present. For example, is the topic something that is worthwhile to communicate? Do you believe in the topic or are you being asked to present a view that opposes your true convictions?

Topic research involves educating yourself thoroughly in the content and subject matter of the presentation. This includes library or Internet research, consulting with subject matter experts (SMEs), and so on. Believe it or not, but public speaking has few hard and fast rules and guidelines that must be followed from topic research through developing the presentation. Despite the lack of hard rules, most experts do agree on one thing: The speaker needs to build on what the audience already knows, understands, believes, and wants.

Starting with what the audience currently knows and building on that information helps you to thwart audience boredom brought on by covering rote information. As a rule, most people aren't eagerly clamoring to hear a speech. Perhaps attendance at the presentation is required for the audience. Or perhaps their reluctance to attend a presentation is due to having endured too many speakers who were self-centered or ill-prepared. Strange as it may seem, this is your first advantage!

Because audience expectations are often low, you may exceed expectations simply by making it clear that you have taken the audience's background and interests into account and are prepared to present your views logically and concisely. Audiences want presenters who demonstrate mastery over the session, focus on the advertised content, demonstrate professional delivery techniques, use facilitation techniques to engage the audience, and know the topic and materials.

The power of advertising also plays a role in setting the appropriate audience expectations long before they walk into the presentation room. The title of a speech or presentation is often one of the best marketing tools that you can develop. Frequently, the title of a presentation is needed immediately—even prior to you creating or refining the presentation—so that the presentation can be publicized and listed in agendas or programs.

When creating the title, work to continually massage and polish it to make it catchy. Some speechwriters prefer to create the title first, whereas others prefer to develop a speech's content in full and then return to develop the title.

POINTER

To attract more attention make your presentation title catchy!

No matter which method is used, the speech and its title should be built around a single theme, and the scope and title should be scaled down to a manageable level. Remember to keep a "truth in advertising" approach during this process. Carefully craft the description of the presentation since audience members evaluate a session on how well it meets their expectations. Many of their expectations are created by program materials. As the presenter, if you have a hand in crafting this information—make it realistic. If you do not have a role in writing the presentation description, then understand what the participants think they have come to hear.

No matter how amazing your presentation skills, your audience will be less than enthused if the title of the presentation does not match the content or if a bit of a "bait and switch" was pulled and the content that they had expected to hear is suddenly different at the start of the presentation.

If you have the time, keep polishing the title. If time is short, then use these guidelines to ensure that the title:

- reflects what is known about the audience
- isn't so broad that an entirely different theme could be attached to it
- is no longer than 10 words—preferably shorter
- above all, if you have promised to talk on a specific topic in the title, then be sure to stick to that topic or risk a very disappointed and annoyed audience.

Key Questions to Determine "What" the Topic and Purpose of the Presentation Are

- How broad or narrow do you need to focus the topic?
- What is the purpose of the presentation—to inform, persuade, facilitate change, or something else?
- Are the goals provided by the sponsor publicly expressed goals, values, and interests of this person or group? How do these square with your own?
- How much time do you need to fill?
- If a set duration isn't predetermined for the presentation, how long should you talk?
- What's the event? An in-house meeting, a professional society conference, or some other occasion such as an awards-presentation dinner?
- Has this event been held before?
- If so, which speakers were popular and why (for example, because of their topics, points of view, or presentation skills)?
- Are audio or videotapes of successful speakers available for your review?

Where: Considering the Environment

The most dynamic presenter can fail in poorly prepared facilities. Even when the presenter is aware of the participants' backgrounds and has conducted comprehensive topic research, the presentation may still fail if, for example, it is delivered in an overcrowded, hot room. Consideration of the physical environment is a crucial part of the planning process. Include the following questions in the presentation analysis to establish a comfortable physical and social environment.

Key Questions to Determine "Where" the Presentation Will Occur

◆ Where is the event being held?

◆ How will you get there? Do you need directions and is parking available, if needed?

◆ How big should the facility be to accommodate the audience?

◆ How will the room or meeting room be set up? Theater-style, runway-style, classroom-style, banquet-style, or other?

◆ Is it an all-purpose meeting room or specially designed for public addresses?

◆ Are breakout rooms available if required?

◆ Are all rooms accessible to all participants?

◆ Are restrooms nearby and are they accessible to all participants, including those with disabilities?

◆ Are the lighting and sound systems appropriate to support a large screen, presentation software, microphones, and dimmable lights?

◆ Will a computer be provided with what you need, or do you need to bring your own setup of presentation software to run the presentation?

◆ Is a podium available? Does it have a light?

◆ Will there be room for a cup of water?

◆ What type of microphone and sound system are available?

◆ Does the microphone lift out of a holder or do you need to wear a lapel mike?

◆ Will you be "stuck" at the podium: If not, how long is the microphone cord to allow movement during the presentation?

Considering the physical environment is crucial to success.

- What will be behind you—a stage, a screen, a curtain, a banner? What color?
- What type of audience distractions does the room have (for example, windows with scenic views, adjacent noisy rooms, a lobby of people coming and going)?
- How do you adjust the temperature of the room and what is the process to make the room warmer or cooler (for example, do you need to call someone or can it be adjusted within the room)?

The ideal presentation room ensures that the audience can listen without distraction in safety and comfort. The audience needs to see and hear. They need ventilation and should be away from smoke fumes or kitchen aromas. Seating should be arranged to maximize the view of the presentation area or stage. Presenters should speak from an area in the front of the room where the audience can hear the message and see their gestures, expressions, and body language.

When: How the Time of Day Affects Presentation Planning

The time of day for delivering the presentation affects not only the structure of the presentation but also the types of activities, breakouts, or facilitation techniques you may need to use to keep the audience actively engaged. For example, plan for high-level activity after lunch and carefully position breaks—especially if you will be presenting for more than an hour.

Key Questions to Determine "When" the Presentation Will Occur

- When is the event?
- What time of the day will you be scheduled to speak?
- How long are you expected to speak or present?
- Who or what immediately precedes and follows you on the agenda?
- Will there be a speaker with an opposing view?

◆ Will you be introduced by someone else?

◆ If so, may you draft your own introduction?

Why: What Action Do You Expect

Although answering the audience analysis questions arms you with more information for creating or tailoring the presentation, keep in mind that another part of the planning equation needs to focus on what you want the audience to do as a result of the presentation.

For example, is this a call to action such as trying to reduce all costs associated with everyday tasks to achieve the organization's profitability goal by the end of the year? Or are you trying to persuade participants on a specific point of view? Perhaps a system implementation is driving the need for the presentation and your role is to help facilitate employee acceptance of the change and the new system.

Key Questions to Identify "Why" the Presentation Opportunity Occurred

◆ Who is sponsoring or holding the event at which you are to speak?

◆ What gave rise to this opportunity to present?

◆ If a topic was provided to you, why that particular topic for the identified audience?

◆ What are participants expected to do as a result of attending the presentation?

◆ Why are participants coming to the presentation—is it mandatory or voluntary?

◆ Is an organization hosting or paying for the presentation? If so, why are they hosting the event (for example, continuing-education needs or mandatory regulatory requirements)?

Worksheet 1.1 provides all the five W key questions in one handy list to make it easy for you to consider your presentation needs so you can begin to formulate your presentation.

WORKSHEET 1.1
Plan Your Presentation

This worksheet will help you get started on planning for a successful presentation. Remember, it does not matter if you are giving a briefing to 10 team members about a new product or company initiative, speaking to 500 attendees at a professional conference, or conducting a one-hour training session for your department on features of a new software package—the same rules apply. Planning and preparation are the keys to success.

Ask the Right Questions

Who is my audience? Determine the WIIFM (see page 7 for a list of key questions to ask).

Key Participant Questions—Do You Know . . .	Answer	Notes
Company positions—higher, lower, the same as you?		
Industry affiliation?		
If your audience will agree with you?		
If attendance is mandatory?		
If the room will be crowded?		
Any personal information about your audience, i.e., leisure activity, hobbies?		
The age range of your audience, i.e.?		
Anything about the racial or ethnic composition?		
Is presentation attendance mandatory?		
The audience's level of knowledge or expertise on the topic?		

continued on next page

Worksheet 1.1, continued

Key Participant Questions—Do You Know . . .	Answer	Notes
What objections are likely?		

What does my audience expect to learn? Research your audience. What did you learn? (See page 11 for key questions on your topic and purpose.)

Key Research Questions— Determine . . .	Answer	Notes
How broad or focused to make your presentation?		
Your purpose—to inform, persuade, facilitate change, something else?		
If the goals and values of your presentation match your audience?		
The type of event—in house, professional conference, and so on		
How much time do you have to speak?		
Event history. How have other speakers succeeded?		
Are audio or videotapes of other successful presentations available?		

continued on next page

Worksheet 1.1, continued

Where and when will the event be held? What logistics am I responsible to coordinate versus someone else? Verify your presentation time, site needs, and the room setup.

Presentation Site & Logistics Questions— Determine. . .	Answer	Notes
The time of day that you are scheduled to speak.		
Who or what immediately precedes or follows you on the agenda (e.g., a speaker with an opposing view?)		
Where is the event?		
How will you get there?		
If you need directions and if parking is available.		
The size of the presentation room.		
The room setup. Can you modify the room setup, if needed?		
If the audiovisual equipment will be provided and what you are responsible to bring (e.g., computer with presentation software, overhead projector, screen, flipcharts, and so on)		
If the room is equipped with dimmable lighting and a sound system to support your presentation needs.		

continued on next page

Presentation Site & Logistics Questions— Determine. . .	Answer	Notes
If a podium is available and if it has a light.		
If there will be room for a cup of water, your notes and handouts or other items (e.g., props).		
If a microphone is available. If so, will you be "stuck" at the podium or able to move freely (e.g., wireless mike or mike with long cord).		
What will be behind you? What color?		
If you will be introduced by someone else and if you may draft your own introduction.		

Why is your topic important to your audience? What unique information do you plan to share with your audience? Why do you think your audience should listen to what you have to say?

Key Audience / Selling You Questions	Answer	Notes
Why should you be making this presentation?		
What benefits can you give your audience?		
Can you create a 30-second elevator speech?		

Determining the Type of Presentation

Along with determining the five Ws, you also need to determine the type of presentation you want to create and present. The word "presentation" means different things depending on the context of the situation—for example, is the presentation a briefing, a speech, a training session, or a conference session? The following descriptions explain each type of presentation and highlight the key differences.

Briefings

A briefing is a condensed, highly focused information session on a specific topic. The goal of a briefing is information transfer, which often involves covering the most information possible in the least amount of time. Briefings often occur in an office or conference room and are delivered to one person or a small group. For example, think of a White House press briefing or a briefing of senior executives on the latest regulatory status for bringing a new product to market. Participants often ask rigorous questions to understand the thoroughness and depth of what they are hearing. Briefings usually include visuals (slides, charts, and models) and handouts of reference materials covering the entire presentation and supplemental information.

Speeches

Speeches provide information with the purpose of inspiring or motivating the audience to act on what they heard, and the topic often reflects a common interest. Audience sizes may range from fewer than 50 to over 1,000 people. Speeches may last 20 to 60 minutes—with 40 minutes as the average. Speeches may also require the presenter to be flexible since time limits may be rigid and speakers may be required to shorten or extend their presentations to fit the agenda. Speakers are often in the spotlight and may use microphones, stages, or platforms to ensure that the participants can see and hear them.

Speeches often occur at organization meetings, conferences, and conventions and at events such as banquets or award ceremonies. They are often held in hotels or conference and convention centers. Speakers use eye contact to help engage the audience, but for large groups, speakers may need to magnify their gestures, voice inflection, and other presentation dynamics.

Training Sessions

Training sessions are structured programs designed to increase knowledge and skills and to promote change. They often take more time to accomplish the goals set than do briefings and speeches. The sessions take place in training rooms, hotels, conference rooms—anywhere that participants can see and hear. In fact, training sessions have even taken place in county court rooms on days when court wasn't in session—the room was the only one available and was large enough to hold all of the participants who needed training. Lengthy training sessions may include breaks and lunch planned at appropriate points in the material. Strong trainers focus the facilitation on the group, two-way communication, and aiding the learning process. Visuals are usually prepared ahead of time as well as on the fly to clarify points, gather ideas from participants, and illustrate processes. To facilitate the transfer of knowledge and skill development, training sessions usually involve exercises, role play, discovery activities, and many other types of active training techniques to engage participants and facilitate the learning process. Handouts and reference materials are often provided for note-taking and posttraining reference.

Conference Sessions

A conference session is often a hybrid, combining the elements of the briefing, training session, and the speech into one program. Since conference sessions usually last for an hour or more, presenters have more time to engage participants with some sharing activities, role play, and exercises related to the information presented. Group size, seating arrangements, and other logistics often dictate the dynamics of the presentation—which need to be carefully planned since they greatly affect the speech. The most successful conference sessions include

- carefully planned content
- a strong opening and closing
- microphone and prepared dynamics (eye contact, voice, variety, pacing, gestures, visuals, and so on)
- an action-planning step either during or at the conclusion of the session.

Preparing Your Elevator Speech

Inevitably at some point in the presentation—usually the beginning—participants will wonder

- Why was this presenter selected?
- What qualities/credentials qualify this person above others?
- What special perspective does this person offer?
- Why is this topic significant?
- What value will I gain compared with the time spent listening?

To create a supportive presentation environment, let the audience know who you are, both professionally and personally. You probably want to be a bit humble and low key when talking about your credentials, but don't be afraid to mention items related to the discussion regarding who you are to help build credibility.

Audiences want presenters who demonstrate mastery in delivering presentations, as well as in the topic of the presentation. Audiences are naturally curious about the presenter and his or her qualifications—so having an elevator speech prepared is imperative.

An elevator speech is a very short introduction of yourself used in situations in which you are meeting a lot of people and are probably not spending a great deal of time with any one of them.

The trick is to make your elevator speech so intriguing that participants will want to sit up and pay attention or will want to spend more time talking with you after the presentation.

A key business tool, an elevator speech is a concise (approximately 1 to 2 minutes), carefully planned, and well-practiced description of the benefits and value that you can provide for multiple purposes—whether during the presentation, or for your organization, the industry, and so on. The term "elevator speech" originated to describe a concise communication that can be delivered in the time that it takes to ride from the top to the bottom of a building in an elevator. This speech is an important tool that can be used every day to network with peers, at career fairs, when talking with current or prospective employers, when meeting and calling on clients, during opportunities with higher-level executives, at job interviews, and when trying to either land a presentation opportunity or during the opening of your presentation.

Develop and Structure Your Presentation

OVERVIEW

- Components of any presentation
- Engaging the audience
- Openings, transitions, and closings
- Creating the presentation outline and body content
- Nine qualities of effective presentations

You probably don't need to *write* a speech because you aren't going to *read* one. You're going to speak about something that perhaps you do every day. For this reason, you need to decide how to grab the audience's attention with the opening, develop and sequence the content, include transitions to help lead the audience through your logic, close the talk, and choose memorable words.

To get started, draft lists, outlines, or "mind maps" of the possibilities before making your final decision. At times there are exceptions to the no-speech-writing rule; put your full speech in writing, if

- ◆ someone else may be called on (at the last minute) to give your speech
- ◆ sponsors of the event demand a copy of the presentation
- ◆ your organization's public relations department's approval is required before you may speak on your organization's behalf
- ◆ you won't feel prepared unless you write it out.

Components of Any Presentation

With the audience analysis in hand, now it is time to put pencil to paper and craft your presentation. But where do you start? Start by planning the end. It's what the audience is most likely to remember that day or even weeks after the presentation.

Imagine what you want the audience to respond to. For example, are you presenting

- ◆ a call to action to help identify and suggest more efficient ways to conduct business
- ◆ a detail or statistic about the topic
- ◆ a declarative statement of the main idea
- ◆ a countdown of items to illustrate the main idea
- ◆ a rhetorical question
- ◆ a command?

Every presentation includes five components:

- ◆ meet/greet
- ◆ opening
- ◆ transition
- ◆ building the body
- ◆ closing.

> **POINTER**
>
> Start planning at the end! Your conclusion is what the audience is most likely to remember.

Use Worksheet 2.1 to help you begin to develop your presentation. It will guide you in structuring the five key components.

Greet and Engage the Audience

Depending on the size of your audience and the environment, make every effort to try to meet and greet the participants as they enter the presentation room. This is a golden opportunity to conduct a mini assessment of "who" is in your audience, why they are attending the presentation, and what they hope to get out of it.

Audience Size and Presentation Considerations

The size of the audience will dictate the type of interaction that you can feasibly build into the structure of the presentation. For example:

◆ **Groups of fewer than 15 people:** This size audience allows for a more intimate presentation and gives you the flexibility to introduce group activities, exercises, discussions, role play, and so on. Consider a more personal approach when preparing for this size group since you will most likely have the opportunity to connect with each audience member at some point during the presentation.

◆ **Groups of 15 to 40:** An audience of this size still offers some flexibility in how you structure and deliver the presentation. You can still make the presentation more interactive but timing needs to be weighed since facilitation discussions or group activities—while often valuable—can gobble up more time than allotted on the agenda.

◆ **Groups larger than 40:** In a group of this size, the dynamics change pretty dramatically. You may need some audio support for everyone to hear you and individual audience introductions may not be feasible to meet the time constraints of the presentation content. You might need to have participants turn to two or three of their peers and introduce themselves instead. Although you will still want to interact with your audience, keep in mind that an audience of this size may not have the ability to ask "unlimited" questions and you may have to take control and refocus the discussion to stay on task to deliver all of the presentation content.

WORKSHEET 2.1

Develop and Structure Your Presentation

This worksheet will help you get started in developing and structuring a successful presentation that provides value to your audience. Remember it does not matter if you are giving a briefing to a small group or a presentation to an auditorium full of people—the main components of every successful presentation are the same.

Presentation Component	Tips	Create Your Presentation Outline & Flow
Meet & Greet:	Greeting audience members when they arrive helps to make them comfortable and provides you with an opportunity to find out more about them and their motivation for attending the presentation. Decide how you plan to "meet" your audience whether it is small and intimate or a large group.	
Openings should: 1. Grab the audience's attention 2. Express the main point 3. Express benefit & WIIFM	Consider using jokes, humorous or relevant stories, anecdotes, icebreakers, brief exercises, an imaginative visual, a provocative statement, a unique demonstration, or a compelling question.	Opening:

Transitions:

Examples:

"First, second . . . "

"To begin, next"

"On the other hand . . . "

"To the contrary"

"As a result . . . "

Transitions:

Create a transition for each key point to segue to different parts of the presentation and to create a cohesive flow in an understandable manner.

Transitions:

1.

2.

3.

4.

5.

Key Points:

1.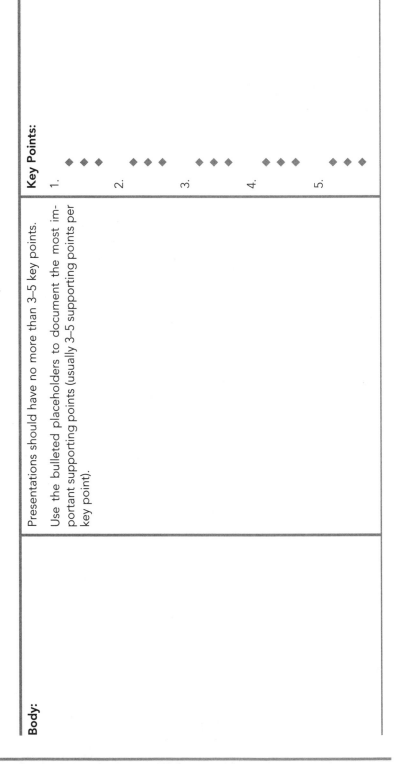

2.

3.

4.

5.

Body:

Presentations should have no more than 3–5 key points.

Use the bulleted placeholders to document the most important supporting points (usually 3–5 supporting points per key point).

Closing:	**Closing:**
Examples:	The end of the presentation is usually what people remember most—so make it memorable.
Brief review	
Key benefits	
Call to action	
Issue a challenge	
Final Q&A	

Presentation Planning Assessment:

Use the presentation assessment questions to determine if the outline and proposed content listed above is on target.

- ☐ Does the presentation content provide value and offer up to five significant insights that audience members can use in their personal lives or back on the job?
- ☐ Do you introduce the key points of the presentation early to keep the audience's attention?
- ☐ Is the presentation material, language, and technical information tailored to meet the specific needs of your audience?
- ☐ Do the presentation's key points unfold in a logical sequence (e.g., time, importance, process flow, or other logical order)?
- ☐ Is the presentation broken into digestible nuggets?
- ☐ Is the content outline appropriate for the length of your presentation?
- ☐ Is each key point backed with facts, visual aids, or anecdotes to make the information memorable?
- ☐ Is the presentation structure logical and geared to the appropriate knowledge level of the audience so that a typical audience member can understand?
- ☐ Does the close end with a bang and accomplish what you want (e.g., a call to action or challenge)?

STEP

2

This will help you to validate your up-front audience analysis information and perhaps gain some insight into hot topics or sticky questions that may come up during your presentation.

For large audiences, you can still conduct this assessment—but rather than talking with individuals, pose your questions to the entire group and have them respond with a show of hands. You could also have them answer a few brief questions and share their responses with their neighbors to get them actively talking, moving around, and engaged before you begin your formal presentation.

No matter how you go about trying to greet and engage the audience, this is a key step in opening with a bang and establishing rapport early in the process.

Openings

An effective opening is crucial to the start of any presentation since it bridges audience members from whatever they were doing before to the topic of the presentation. The opening needs not only to establish the credibility of the presenter but should also accomplish three things:

- ◆ grab the audience's attention
- ◆ express the main point of the presentation
- ◆ state the benefit and explain what the audience can expect to get out of the presentation.

POINTER

A successful presentation begins by grabbing the audience's attention. If you grab them early you will keep them engaged.

As you begin putting pencil to paper to craft your opening, think about ways of grabbing your audience's attention. You can do this by focusing on the purpose of your presentation and expressing the benefit the audience will receive from hearing your presentation. Don't worry if you can't immediately develop a stunning opening. Some presenters prefer to wait until they've written the entire presentation before trying to develop a catchy opener.

For example, compare these two openings:

"I want to talk to you about the importance of ensuring that our corporate initiatives are valued and focused on supporting the organizational strategy."

"A major issue that we face today is how to consistently demonstrate value to our internal and external customers to achieve our organizational goals. I'm going to discuss a practical approach to do just that—which will enable you to use your power to influence the strategic direction of the organization."

Which of these openings grabs your attention? The second example tells the audience not only the topic of the presentation but also expresses the benefit they will receive if they stay and listen. It also clearly and enthusiastically states the WIIFM (what's in it for me) for the audience, something that always gets people's attention.

The second example is written from the perspective of the audience members and emphasizes the value they will get out of the presentation—instead of from the perspective of the presenter. Although not all openings for each presentation you do are going to sound the same, the opening you choose sets the stage and tone for the presentation and is often a determining factor of whether the audience will be tuned in or not. If you grab them early, you'll keep them engaged. If you don't, it's awfully difficult to get them back.

Some other types of openers include

◆ **Jokes**—some presenters like to lighten the mood by telling a joke. A joke can work if people find you funny and if you don't cross the line between good taste and bad. A general rule for joke-telling is if you have a question whether it would be appropriate to tell it, then don't.

◆ **Humorous or relevant stories or anecdotes**—a story or anecdote can work well as an opening remark, but both require practice because few people are natural storytellers.

◆ **An icebreaker or brief exercise**—an icebreaker is a brief exercise that often serves as a means for audience members to introduce themselves and to get to know each other. An icebreaker can be an effective way of starting your presentation provided that it's appropriate for the audience you are presenting to and you have enough time to do it.

◆ **A question**—you can ask either a rhetorical question ("How would you like to learn how to become more credible in order to influence your organization in achieving its strategic goals?"), or you can ask a real question ("How many people find they have at least a little influence in their organization?"). In the former, you are not looking for a response, and in the latter you may simply call for a show of hands.

Openings should both explain the topic of the presentation and capture the audience's attention. Do not attempt the second without covering the first. Remember, if your attention-grabber does not tie into the topic, you will only confuse and distract the audience. Here are some best practices for openings:

◆ State the purpose or goal of the presentation. All audiences want to know the objective(s).

◆ Make the opening relevant to real-life experiences. This helps participants grasp the content of the presentation by relating it to something they understand.

◆ Ask questions to stimulate thinking on the topic of the presentation. Besides stimulating the thought process, this technique helps participants develop a focus on the topic. These might be rhetorical questions or a show of hands.

◆ Share a personal experience or anecdote that is universal. You will spark participant interest if they have experienced something similar. But limit your "war" stories; too many can turn off interest.

Seven "Sinful" Statements

The following opening statements usually cause audiences to groan:

♦ "Well, they put this platform on the stage up here for me, but I feel so much more natural and comfortable down here on the floor, so I think I'll just speak from here." (The people in the back can't see the speaker.)

♦ "These microphones always feel so awkward. I'll bet you can all hear me if I talk real loud. Raise your hand if you can't hear me." (This speaker drops his or her voice volume after six seconds and many can't hear.)

♦ "Let's get into groups of eight or 10 and spend 15 minutes on what you want to get out of our time here today." (Interaction in large groups requires a totally different structure than is appropriate for a large presentation.)

♦ "I don't have any handouts for you today, but if each of you will leave me your business card, I'll get something for you." (Many attendees see this as a way to build the presenter's mailing list for potential sales calls and wonder why he or she didn't prepare ahead of time.)

♦ "In our short time here today, I don't have time to take you through our whole process, so I'll just show you the first three steps and you can follow up later if you want more information." (Why didn't the presenter select a topic he or she could cover fully in the time allowed?)

♦ "I know it says the program I'm here to talk about is _____, but I submitted that topic eight months ago and now I need to change to another focus." (Attendees recognize this as the traditional "bait and switch.")

♦ "They just called me yesterday to ask if I could fill in for the regional director, who got a last-minute contract with a client. . . . Now, let's see, what's the topic?"

- Create interest with an imaginative visual. Weekend comic strips or editorial pages are full of motivational tools. Remember to check the copyright laws, and if necessary, ask artists for permission to use their work.
- Make a provocative statement. When applicable, this technique generates comments and discussion to help introduce your topic. Be careful with this one! It can also turn off your audience if not handled well.
- Give a unique demonstration. This works well with technical topics. You can then proceed from the introduction to explanations of the "why" and "how" of the demonstration.
- Use an interesting or famous quotation, or perhaps turn this quotation around just a bit to fit the topic. For example: "Ask not what work teams can do for you, but what you can do for your work team."
- Relate the topic to previously covered content. Perhaps the speaker who preceded you has established the groundwork for your presentation topic.

Transitions

Transitions help you move from point to point in a smooth, flowing manner. They are segues to the different parts of your presentation and are important in making your presentation cohesive and understandable. Because people don't speak the way they write, try developing transitions using language you are comfortable with to connect the pieces of what you've written in your notes. For example, a transition based on the example used in this chapter might sound like this: "Another example of establishing your credibility in your organization is understanding the business your business is in . . . "

Help audience members to follow the sequence and flow of the presentation by using transitional expressions such as:

- first . . . second . . . third
- to begin . . . next . . . and finally
- at the start . . . then . . . afterward

- early on . . . later . . . eventually . . . now
- meanwhile
- and . . . plus . . . also.

If you are building arguments or counterarguments, use expressions such as:

- on the other hand
- by the same token
- to the contrary
- so
- as a result
- despite
- similarly
- even if
- even so.

Creating the Presentation Outline and Body Content

The body of the presentation should specifically support the purpose and main point of the presentation and meet the needs of the audience, based on your research. Normally, this is achieved by using supporting points. These points reinforce the purpose and the main point. Because most people only remember a small part of the presentation, you'll want to limit the supporting points to a manageable number—somewhere between three and five of the most important ones.

When structuring the body content, go back to the research that you've done about your audience's needs and the purpose of the presentation. Write down what you perceive to be the most important points that support in some way the presentation's purpose and main point. Write some

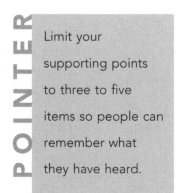

POINTER

Limit your supporting points to three to five items so people can remember what they have heard.

notes that fully express each supporting point, but don't worry initially about how you are going to say it.

Next, review your notes and begin to pare down the supporting points to three to five strong ones. Once you have decided what they are, begin writing your notes. Do this in the way that seems to work best for you. Try writing two or three iterations each time, trimming down the wording so that eventually you get to the talking points you feel comfortable with. Remember, you don't want a script or anything lengthy.

Some presenters prefer to use an outline format in which headings trigger your talking points for the presentation. Others want the comfort of having substantial notes to draw from. Beware when taking this approach because too many words are an invitation to read your notes verbatim. However, if you're going to err on one side, it probably makes more sense to have more information in your notes, at least initially in your career as a presenter, because copious notes can serve as a security blanket. It's also always easier to take information away than to add it later.

After the main points and subpoints of the speech are documented, decide how the ideas should be sequenced to flow from beginning to end. For example,

◆ main topic to details of who, what, when, where, why, and how
◆ problem to solution
◆ chronological (time) or spatial order
◆ details added up to a conclusion
◆ arguments against your contention, then counterarguments for your contention
◆ setting up a rule, then describing its exceptions
◆ listing possibilities, then reaching your preference through a process of elimination.

Let's look at how the opening and transition used earlier in this chapter might now be structured when developing and segueing into the body content:

◆ **Opening:** "A major issue that we face today is how to consistently demonstrate value to our internal and external customers in order to achieve our organizational goals. I'm going to discuss a practical approach to do just that— which will enable you to use your power to influence the strategic direction of the organization."

P O I N T E R

Additional Considerations When Structuring the Presentation

◆ **Audience Expertise**

Knowing how much knowledge or expertise your audience has regarding the subject of your presentation is a key piece of information required to effectively structure the presentation. This information will influence the breadth and depth of your presentation. You will need to determine if the audience needs to hear everything you are prepared to present or if you should employ the KISS principle ("keep it simple, stupid!). If the audience expertise varies widely, try to approach the topic from a middle-ground perspective so that you provide new information to novices and sprinkle in more advanced information for those who already have some knowledge of the topic. You can always adjust the pace and depth of the presentation to a level that ensures you are reaching as many people as possible.

◆ **Presenting to Superiors**

Structure the presentation to involve your organizational superiors by asking them to share personal experiences about the topic, for example, which leadership traits they find most useful in their roles as managers. By establishing and encouraging this dynamic, you assume a facilitator role that builds credibility, shows off your skills, and takes the pressure off you for being the sole source of content and ideas.

◆ **Transition:** "This requires you to establish credibility by implementing the following three practices . . . (supporting points):
   1. knowing your business
   2. acting strategically
   3. understanding your organization's culture.
◆ **Body of 1st point:** Let's take a look at each of the three, starting with the first—knowing your business . . . "

You then elaborate on each of the supporting points, making sure that what you say explains and supports the main point and purpose of the presentation.

Nine Qualities of Effective Presentations

When developing the body of your presentation, keep in mind that effective presentations demonstrate each of these nine qualities:

◆ **Value**—Audiences expect substance. They want value for the time and money that they or their organizations have invested. Participants seek insights the presenter has gleaned from his or her accomplishments and experiences on how to succeed. Most presentations offer up to five significant insights that audience members can use back on the job. The presenter makes the insights easily accessible and structures the information for appropriate and timely use. Presentations lacking value seem pointless.

◆ **Clarity**—The key points of the presentation are introduced early in the speech. These key points guide the speaker in selecting what to include so that the audience receives "pearls" of wisdom rather than a data dump of unorganized information. Presenters lacking clarity seem boring and tend to ramble.

◆ **Tailored**—The material, language, technical information, and examples demonstrate an awareness of current issues and information of interest to this specific audience. The more the speaker can tailor a presentation to a specific audience, the more he or she helps each audience member to consider the possibilities of the topic being presented.

◆ **Logical**—The presentation's key points unfold in a logical sequence (following time, importance, geography, or any other appropriate order). The presenter arranges ideas around a central theme, a metaphor, a model, or some other device to help listeners understand and remember what they hear. Presentations without a logical order seem haphazard and make it difficult for the audience to understand the point.

◆ **Length**—The presenter assumes that his or her listeners have short attention spans. Although effective presentations can run from 30 minutes to several hours, the best presenters break the content into "digestable" nuggets.

◆ **Memorable**—A memorable speech blends general information, proven and practical guidelines, and concrete illustrations and examples. Each key idea is backed with facts, visual aids, anecdotes, or other elements that help audience members remember and apply what they have heard. Presentations that aren't memorable are mediocre at best.

◆ **Understandable**—Complex, technical, or abstract material is presented in a way that a typical member of the audience can understand. For technical professionals presenting to nontechnical listeners, this requires careful "translation." A true master speaker is one who can communicate the complexities clearly, enabling others to comprehend the subject without baffling with detail. These masters don't talk down to nontechnical audiences. Metaphors, examples, puzzles, props, or models help the audience grasp the basics. Presentations that are overly technical or simplistic may bore or overwhelm the audience.

◆ **Realistic**—The speaker carefully researches the audience before the presentation to have the maximum impact on the group without trying to accomplish too much. Know the audience and always start where they are. Remember that audience members arrive at a presentation with their own concerns. The audience usually responds better if the speaker demonstrates some sensitivity to their concerns.

◆ **Challenging**—An effective presenter closes with a call to action, a challenge, a way to bring the listeners back to the heart of the topic the group was assembled to explore. Presentations lacking this quality seem pointless, lackluster, and boring.

POINTER

Purr and Snarl Words

Words listed as synonyms in a thesaurus can convey different implications. Some purr with approval, whereas their counterparts snarl with disagreement, anger, or sarcasm. Audiences often accept disagreement and righteous anger, but sarcasm rarely wins their hearts or minds.

Purr	Snarl
clever	crafty/sly
unique	odd
easy/plain	simplistic
thrifty/inexpensive	cheap
new	untried/unproven
tried/tested	old-fashioned
quick/speedy	hasty
change from	abandon
open to change	uncertain/unsettled
change	upheaval
challenging	difficult
cautious/gradual	timid/half-hearted
bold	foolhardy
estimate	guess
inaccurate	lie
interpret	distort

Adding Sizzle

Sizzle is a quality that can add greatly to a presenter's effectiveness. Sizzle can consist of storytelling, vision, humor, surprise, emotion, music, drama, dance, lighting, "show-biz," or any other carefully crafted element of communication. Most presentations are adequate without sizzle, but magic can happen when a presenter cares enough to add just the right amount of pizzazz to enthrall an audience.

Many presenters are hesitant to experiment with adding sizzle. They are afraid to look foolish or too casual with important topics. Sometimes caring enough about a subject and an audience to play with the idea is one of the best endorsements presenters can make.

The two segments of the presentation where sizzle is most often used are in the opening and the closing. These segments carry the burdens of attracting the listener and of sending the listener away with valuable insights. They are, therefore, the segments that deserve the highest level of care and attention. Experienced speakers often memorize exactly what they'll say in the first or last two to four minutes of the presentation.

Closings

The end of your presentation is usually what people remember most, so it is important to make your ending a memorable one. An effective closing serves to

- provide a brief review and highlight all key points
- possibly provide a quick review of the benefits the audience got from your presentation
- if appropriate, ask for a call to action of some kind

- ◆ fuel audience actions by giving them a sense of power and purpose
- ◆ consider asking the audience if they have any questions.

NOTES

_____

_____

_____

_____

_____

_____

_____

_____

_____

_____

_____

_____

_____

_____

_____

_____

_____

_____

_____

_____

_____

_____

STEP 2

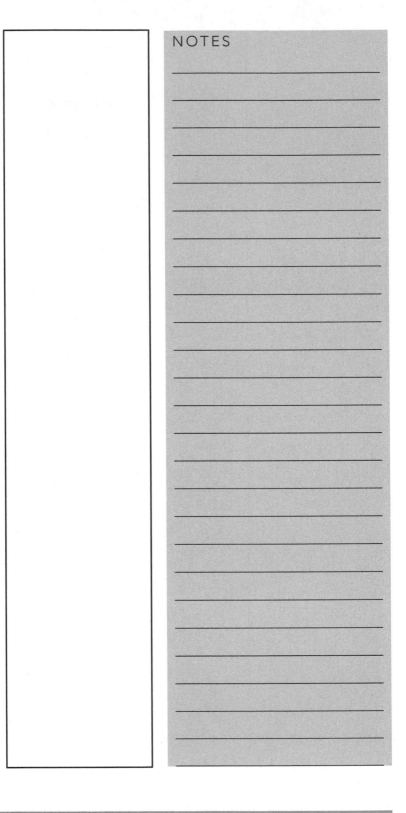

Create Appropriate Visual Aids

Chances are, you'll use at least one visual aid to support your presentation. Visual aids help to make bland presentations come to life—and as the saying goes, sometimes a picture is worth 1,000 words. Keep in mind that sometimes visual aids can have the opposite effect and turn a presentation into a disaster if they are not used effectively.

You've probably attended a presentation at one time during which it was clear that the presenter just learned how to add animation and sound to slides in the presentation—so much so that every time something appeared on the slide, it "flew in" or "checker-boarded across" the screen and emitted a zipping, zapping, or cha-ching noise.

Because most people have an easier time remembering something they have seen, presentations usually benefit from some use of audiovisual support. All visuals and materials should be carefully prepared ahead of time to reflect the professionalism of the speaker, and the presenting organization, and to convey respect for the audience. Therefore, it is important to plan and prepare visual aids carefully to support the presentation and not distract from it.

Benefits of Visual Aids

If you're not quite convinced about the power that visual aids can add, consider this fact. In one study, a presentation that delivered information only verbally achieved a 7 percent comprehension rate; the addition of visuals raised comprehension to 87 percent.

In addition to helping your audience understand and remember your message, visual aids also

◆ Help you to control the flow and structure of the information to maintain and peak the audience's attention as you reveal the key points

◆ Help you to communicate your message quicker and more efficiently

◆ Enable the audience to see what something looks like, clarify relationships among numerical data, show the organizational structure of information, and so on

◆ Provide more clarity when they are organized and thoughtfully integrated

◆ Add interest, variety, and excitement to what might otherwise be a boring presentation.

So which visual aid should you use based on the type of presentation you need to deliver?

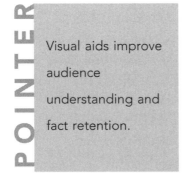

Visual aids improve audience understanding and fact retention.

Determining Which Visual Aid(s) Meets Your Needs

There are many types of visual aids to choose from when planning your presentation. You can use whiteboards, posters, flipcharts, transparencies and overhead projectors, slides, presentation software, and so on. There are advantages and disadvantage to each type of visual aid and some of them lend themselves to specific circumstances more than others. Which type of visual aid you choose will depend on the presentation goals, the makeup of your audience, and your budget. The following questions will help you to select the appropriate visual aid.

- ◆ What is the audience's learning profile? Consider their current level of expertise, motivation for attending the presentation (that is, is it required or optional), and their expectation. You need to ensure that your presentation is informative but that it does not go over their heads.
- ◆ Will sound, motion, color, or other effects be required to present the message effectively? If you only need to highlight specific points, a transparency or text slides might be sufficient.
- ◆ Under what conditions is the presentation taking place? What will be the room size, audience size, and availability of equipment?
- ◆ Do you have the resources—time, money, expertise, and support—to develop a presentation that uses the appropriate visual aids to their best advantage?

So with these initial questions in mind, let's look at a few myths and truths to remember when integrating visual aids into any presentation.

Visual Aid Myths, Facts, and Guidelines

No matter what type of visual aid you plan to use, you can proactively avoid some pitfalls by keeping the following myths, facts, and guidelines in mind when adding visuals to a presentation.

Myths and Facts

Let's dispel some common myths:

- ◆ **Myth 1: The more visual aids used, the better.**
  Fact: The use of visual aids should *support* your presentation but not *be* your presentation. Avoid overdoing the

visuals at the expense of the message. Content is key—
and too many visuals that are not relevant to the content
will only confuse and frustrate the audience.

◆ **Myth 2: Any visual aid is better than none.**
Fact: A visual aid that is too complex to understand is
best left out of the presentation. Visuals should reinforce
and support the message and be of high-enough quality to
clearly reproduce on the presentation materials and
handouts.

◆ **Myth 3: Visual aids are complex and add one more element to worry about in the presentation.**
Fact: Not true. Most problems occurring in presentations
are caused by a lack of preparation. While you will want to
check the equipment and run through the visual aids in advance of the presentation, visuals often help the audience
to readily grasp key concepts and follow the flow of the
presentation.

Guidelines for Using Visual Aids

Use these guidelines to ensure that your visuals support and clarify
presentation content.

◆ **Illustrate only one point per visual**—effective visuals
help the audience to get the point about five seconds after
they appear. As a best practice, show the visual, pause a
moment to let the audience scan the visual and begin to
process the information, and then discuss the presentation
content.

◆ **Use the appropriate number of visuals**—as a guideline,
use only three visuals every five or six minutes to highlight the key points since too many visuals can cause confusion and overload the audience.

◆ **Avoid redundant information**—do not read the exact
same text aloud that appears on a visual. Visual aids
should *complement* your message.

◆ **Keep the design of visuals consistent throughout the
presentation**—when preparing your visual aids, use the

same color scheme to project a unified method and to avoid confusing the audience with arbitrary changes.

◆ **Maintain orientation of the visuals**—try to keep all visuals positioned in a horizontal format since the bottom of the screen is often difficult to see for some audience members.

◆ **Position text in the same location**—on each visual keep the focus in the same place, for example, one-fifth of the way from the top.

◆ **Repeat key information at the beginning and the end**—the beginning and end of the presentation should be an identical summary of the presentation's key points. This not only orients the audience to what is to come, but also helps to close the loop and ensure that you haven't missed any information when reviewing the key points at the end of the presentation.

◆ **Prepare visuals early**—allow enough time to plan and develop visuals that effectively support the presentation. Practice with the visuals until you are comfortable. Avoid making any last-minute changes to visuals since this often increases a presenter's stress level and leaves room for misspellings or other errors to creep into the presentation.

◆ **Talk to the audience, not the visual**—be sure that everyone can see the visual. Talk about the visual aid only while you are showing it and don't leave the visual in view after you have finished talking about it.

Steps for Adding Visual Aids

So what is a good approach to use to get started in planning and developing the presentation visuals? First, visual aids should never happen haphazardly or appear just for decoration. When this happens the visuals tend to distract more than help to convey the message or maintain interest. Use these steps to plan your content.

POINTER

Be consistent in your design and check your spelling. Small errors lead to big distractions.

1. Begin by outlining your presentation, identifying the key and supporting points.

2. Then determine which of these points will need a visual for clarity.

3. Make a thumbnail sketch of each visual.

4. Take a critical look at your outline and the visuals that you have planned. As a general rule, if the visual is not contributing to the clarity or flow of the information, or does not convey the "need to know" information, then throw it out.

5. Experiment with the remaining visuals to add creativity and clarity to support the presentation content.

STEP 3

POINTER

Effective Use of Color

Although color is an attention-getter, if used inappropriately it can be a big distracter. Overall, keep colors consistent throughout the presentation and use color in moderation. Random use of color will confuse rather than enhance your message. Some other factors to consider when choosing whether and how to use color in your presentation include the following:

◆ Use color to organize content, especially in long presentations to highlight the transition from one major segment to another.

◆ Use bright colors to attract attention to major points.

◆ Use contrasting colors to illustrate contrasting concepts or to suggest a major change.

◆ Use colors that contrast enough to be read easily, for example, a dark background with light-colored text, and a conservative color work best.

◆ Use shades of the same color to suggest minor changes.

Mastering Different Types of Visual Aids

Presenters have myriad visual aids available that clearly communicate the presentation's key points, which will help develop a creative and engaging presentation. For example, flipcharts, whiteboards, and overhead transparencies enable you to draw and write on the fly. Presentation software enables you to create formal, structured, professional-looking presentations. High-tech visual aids such as videotape, digital video disks (DVDs), photographic slides, and digital slides can demonstrate or convey information and add a "wow" factor to your presentation. Despite all of these solutions for enhancing your presentation—you need to keep in mind that not all of these options are appropriate all of the time. Visual aids should be used to enhance and convey the message of your presentation—not dominate the entire show.

Flipcharts

A flipchart is the most basic visual aid, usually consisting of an easel and large pads of paper attached to the stand or a cardboard backing. You can purchase a variety of flipchart paper—including ones with sticky backs that act like large Post-it notes that can be displayed around the room. Other varieties of flipchart paper include blank pages, lined pages, or even grids. Flipcharts are a great resource for smaller group presentations and for capturing key points from brainstormed sessions or illustrating information on the fly to help clarify the presentation message.

Using the Touch, Turn, Talk Method

When presenting using a flipchart, stand to one side. Which side depends on which hand you write with. For example, if you are right-handed, stand on the left side of the flipchart (as the audience faces it). If you are using tabs to help you navigate within the mass of flipchart pages, position the tabs on the left side as well (again, as the audience faces the chart). If you are left-handed, then reverse this stance and placement.

When you present using flipcharts as a visual aid, use the "touch, turn, talk" method. To do this:

1. Lightly touch the flipchart page that you are referring to or write something on the page before you begin speaking.
2. Turn toward the audience.
3. Begin speaking to the audience—not to the flipchart.

If you see audience members craning their necks to see the flipchart, that is your cue to move or to position the flipchart so that everyone can see it more readily.

Don't read word for word from the flipchart. The audience can read for themselves. Each page of the flipchart should outline the key and supporting points that you elaborate. The best presenters use visual aids to support the presentation—not be the presentation.

10 Rules When Creating Flipcharts

Consider the following when creating flipcharts:
1. Use a maximum of six lines per page. Use only eight to 10 words per point, and use key words or phrases instead of full sentences. Busy flipcharts obscure your message.
2. Make your letters at least two inches high and verify that the audience can read them from the back of the room.
3. Use headings on each page to orient the audience to the key and supporting points. For example, use bold, capital letters in one color for all headings, and show supporting points as bulleted items in a different color. To make perfect-looking bullets, some presenters use round, colorful stickers.
4. Use three to four different colors to make flipcharts eye-catching and easy to read. Use nontoxic, water-based markers because they smell better, won't bleed through walls and tables, and won't ruin your clothes.
5. If you have to tape flipcharts to a wall for additional writing space, leave one or two blank flipchart pages behind the one you plan to write on to ensure that the marker won't bleed through the paper onto the paint or wallpaper. As a best practice, you can leave a blank sheet of

paper between your written flipchart pages so that the audience cannot see what is ahead on subsequent pages.

6. Use colors that are easy for the audience to see—for example, black and blue tend to be the most visible. Use your judgment about adding green or red for emphasis. These are great colors to imply "do" and "don't" or "positives" and "negatives," but red can be difficult to see from a distance and some audience members might be colorblind and unable to make the distinction.

7. At the top corner of each page closest to where you will be standing, write a brief heading of what's on the next page lightly in pencil with an arrow under it. This note will help you move seamlessly to the material on the following page.

8. Number each page of your flipchart, then mark the corresponding number in your notes to help you quickly get back on track if you get distracted or lose your place.

9. Always check the spelling of your flipcharts.

10. Use Post-It notes, sticky tabs, or clear tape to form tabs at the side of each sheet to make it easy to find the specific flipchart page you want to easily navigate to. Be sure to flag all of the flipchart pages.

Advantages of Using Flipcharts

As a guideline, use flipcharts when:

◆ **You want to capture participant ideas and comments—** while professional-looking flipcharts can be created by hand (if you have good hand-writing) or printed on large blotters, most presenters can create effective flipcharts with little effort. For example, use flipcharts during project team meetings to list the top project issues and to facilitate a brainstorming session during which you capture the possible solutions on a separate flipchart.

◆ **Audience and room size are appropriate**—flipcharts are ideal in rooms with 30 or fewer participants when the chart is positioned so that everyone has a good line of sight. You need the flexibility to display the flipcharts created before the presentation as well as a public place to capture ideas and questions generated during the presentation.

◆ **You have a late-afternoon presentation**—flipcharts are especially helpful for presentations conducted immediately after lunch or in the late afternoon since you do not need to dim the lights to see them as you would for a slide presentation.

◆ **You have little or no budget**—flipcharts are a perfect choice when a last-minute presentation has made its way onto your calendar and you have little time or budget to prepare a presentation. With flipcharts, you can create the key points, graphs, charts, or other information for your presentation at almost any time or anywhere and if on a limited budget.

◆ **You need a crutch**—since flipcharts can be created on the fly, many presenters also use them as a crutch to post an "agenda" of the presentation so that they can glance at the flipchart as a reminder of the next point or topic to discuss. Other presenter tricks include writing in pencil on the corners of blank flipchart pages so that only the presenter can see the key notes he or she wants to discuss—to the audience it appears as if the material comes from the top of his or her head.

◆ **You want to display the visual during the entire presentation**—flipcharts are particularly effective when you want to display a visual, graph, or chart during the entire presentation for you or the participants to refer back to from time to time.

When Not to Use Flipcharts

As a guideline, avoid flipcharts when:

◆ **The size of the room or audience is not appropriate**—although you'd this think would be an obvious error—you've probably seen a presenter writing on a flipchart in a room of 100+ people. The audience will not be able to readily see the flipchart, so choose another visual aid for large group presentations.

◆ **You need to be more formal or professional**—think of conducting a sales presentation for a new client on a flipchart. This medium might not be as formal or professional as you want to be in some situations.

◆ **If your handwriting is barely legible**—try printing in block letters using flipchart paper with lines or a grid as a guide. If the audience can't read your writing, then try another visual aid. The bottom line is that if you do not include flipcharts in your presenter toolkit, then you are depriving yourself—and your audience—of a very useful and unique visual aid.

◆ **If you present the same program regularly**—unless you are going to have your flipcharts laminated, they may get tattered and ragged after several presentations. Laminating flipcharts can be expensive.

Overhead Transparencies

Another useful visual aid is the overhead transparency. Transparencies are similar to flipcharts in that they are low-tech, easy to use, and can be created in a hurry. Colored pens enable you to highlight key points or important words and you can make these decisions on the fly.

Transparencies, however, do require a projector, a projection screen, and electricity, so they are definitely a step up from flipcharts on the technology scale. Because some overhead projectors can project plain paper on the screen—meaning no transparencies are needed—you'll need to verify the type of projector that will be available before you show up for your presentation.

Using Overhead Transparencies

If the room is small, consider positioning the screen and overhead projector facing one corner rather than straight forward. You'll need to arrange for this room setup in advance.

Depending on the placement of the projector cord, you might want to use duct tape to tape it to the floor to prevent a tripping hazard.

Before the presentation, ensure that the projector is focused so that the audience can see the entire image clearly. If you want to check the focus without revealing your images, place a coin with ridges (quarter or dime) on the glass and adjust the focus.

Keep the projector's surface clean since every bit of dirt and dust is magnified about 100 times when it is projected on the screen.

The whirr of an overhead projector fan is often a bit noisy, so remember to project your voice and verify that everyone in the audience can hear you at the start of your presentation.

Use a flat-sided pointer, like a pencil, to indicate the images you are discussing since it will enable you to cleanly point out certain parts of the image and will not roll off the flat surface of the projector when you lay it down.

Use the "revelation" technique to reveal each point on the transparency one at a time by using a piece of paper under the transparency. (If you put the paper on top of the transparency, it will slip off the moment you take your fingers away from it.)

Talk to the audience—not the projector.

Know how to turn off the projector and do so when changing transparencies (or you will blind the audience) or whenever you are not using a transparency as a visual aid.

To prolong the life of the projector bulb and to prevent it from breaking due to the heat generated, run the fan for a few minutes after turning off the lamp.

Either carry an emergency bulb with you or know how to contact the audiovisual technician at the presentation site in case the projector bulb burns out. A spare bulb is often stored in a compartment inside the projector itself.

Advantages of Using Overhead Transparencies

As a guideline, use overhead transparencies when:

◆ **Your presentation is informal or in a small room—** although you can have transparencies professionally made, overhead transparencies are best suited for an informal, small-group presentation. Sometimes transparencies are easier for the audience to see than flipcharts.

◆ **Your budget is small or time is short**—transparencies can be made easily and are less expensive than slides.

◆ **You want to project existing materials to a group—** some transparencies are compatible with inkjet or laser printers. For example, you can print samples of forms, organizational charts, or graphics from your computer directly onto a transparency. Other transparencies can be loaded right into photocopiers so that you can create transparencies of anything that you can copy (for example, pages out of a book).

◆ **You want to add to your presentation on the fly—** grease pencils and transparency markers enable you to write or emphasize a point during the presentation.

◆ **You will give the presentation several times—** transparencies are easier to transport and are a little more durable than flipcharts. Some transparencies even come three-hole punched to easily organize and store in a binder to carry with you.

When Not to Use Overhead Transparencies

As a general rule, avoid using overhead transparencies when:

◆ **The presentation site is too small to contain a projector, a screen, and the audience**—overhead projectors can be quite bulky and at times interfere with the audience's line of sight.

◆ **Making a formal presentation**—for all of their benefits, overhead transparencies are usually considered a step up in quality from a flipchart, especially if you have them professionally produced. However, for formal presentations, you should use PowerPoint or other presentation software or slides.

10 Rules to Follow When Creating Overhead Transparencies
Consider the following when creating overhead transparencies:

1. More is not always better. Keep the information on each transparency to a maximum of six lines with no more than eight words per line.
2. If making transparencies from a computer printer or a photocopier, remember to make the size of the text large enough for the audience to easily see. Choose a clear and easy-to-ready type face that has a font size of at least 24 points.
3. When choosing colors, apply the same principles as those outlined for flipcharts.
4. Use headings on each page to distinguish among key points and use bulleted lists to denote supporting points.
5. Be consistent with the font, colors, and formatting of headings, key points and supporting points throughout all the transparencies for the presentation.
6. Keep some transparency markers in your toolkit since all markers are not created equal. Test them before you use them for a presentation.
7. Number each transparency on the border as well as on the actual transparency. You'll be glad you did if you drop them!
8. Write a number on each transparency to correspond with your notes so that you can seamlessly transition from one visual aid to another during your speech.
9. Always check your spelling.
10. If you are going to hand-write the transparencies, make sure that your handwriting is legible. If not, consider

making the transparencies by printing them from a computer or using presentation software.

PowerPoint or Other Presentation Software

PowerPoint and other types of software-presentation tools have become so prevalent that they deserve their own discussion in the visual-aid category. Where overhead projectors and transparencies were once a staple of presentations, presentation software now reigns as the premier presentation tool in many organizations.

Presentation software enables you to create digital slides that can be shown to an audience in a number of ways including:

- on a desktop computer or liquid crystal diode (LCD) display on a laptop computer for small groups
- on a digital projector that interfaces directly with a laptop or PDA (special accessory required)
- using a computer projector that projects images directly from your monitor onto a screen or flat surface for larger groups
- using an overhead projector that uses specially made transparencies
- over the Internet or an organization's intranet
- on hard copies of slides that can be distributed as handouts.

Presentation software offers many advantages over transitional visual aids, for example, its ease of use and the ability to capture "speaker's notes" on each slide so that you can either print your "script," which shows the slide image and your speaking notes, or it can display your speaking notes on the slide—which is only visible to you during the presentation.

Advantages of Using Presentation Software

As a guideline, use presentation software when:

- **Your presentation is formal**—presentation software tools are not only easy to use, but they also enable you to produce high-quality, professional-looking presentations. You can quickly rearrange the order of the slides and add movement, animation, and sound to each slide.

◆ **You conduct the same presentation regularly**—because presentations created using presentation software can be saved to a disk, CD-ROM, jump drive, laptop, or even a PDA, your presentation is easily stored, backed up, and transported. This means no bulky slide trays or flimsy transparencies.

◆ **You need flexibility to modify your presentation**—presentation software enables you to quickly add or replace slides using your keyboard. This means that you can easily tweak the content for different audiences and rearrange the flow of the presentation or the order of the key and supporting points to continually improve on the presentation and delivery.

◆ **It is appropriate for audiences of all sizes**—presentations created using this tool are professional-looking and are just as appropriate for one or two people sitting around a table, as a presentation for C-level executives, or to large groups in a conference center.

◆ **You want to reveal information in a specific manner**—when conducting a presentation, presentation software is especially adept at helping you to "reveal" the information that you want—when you want—to help maintain and peak the audience's interest. Presentation software includes "builds," which enable you to display all points on a slide, or with the click of your mouse or keyboard, to reveal just the current point that is being discussed. This feature even "dims" the previous talking points on the slide so that all information discussed on that slide is still visible to the audience, but the current point being discussed is highlighted in a different color. This helps to orient the audience not only to where they have been, but the current topic of discussion in case they "take a mental holiday" during the presentation.

When Not to Use Presentation Software

With all of the advantages of presentation software—is there ever a time when you should not use this tool for presentations? As a general rule, do not use presentation software when:

- **Your presentation needs flexibility**—the presentation and the slides you create with the software are usually designed to deliver a particular message in a structured way. For example, you've given your sales presentation to explain your products, services, and the industries you serve. That type of scenario works great for structured presentations using presentation software. However, now it is time to listen to the customer's business needs and to discover where you might have a solution to meet those needs. A structured presentation does not lend itself to this type of discussion during which you need flexibility to ask probing questions and to take the conversation in different directions to be able to understand the full potential of a sales opportunity and the scope of the project.

- **You're fearful of new technology**—if you feel a little "technology challenged," you might want to avoid using presentation software unless you have adequate time to practice using the tool and rehearsing your presentation. If you are not comfortable using the technology, you might be distracted by concerns over pressing the right button to advance slides or to get special animation to appear on the screen rather than delivering a clear, confident presentation.

10 Rules to Follow When Creating Presentations Using Presentation Software

Here are 10 rules to apply when using presentation software:

1. Keep the design clean.
2. Don't add too many effects.
3. Keep the background subtle.
4. Use clip art sparingly.
5. Use the right graph style for the data.
6. Limit colors to three per slide.

7. Adhere to the six-by-six format: No more than six words per line and no more than six lines per slide.
8. Use light colors on dark backgrounds.
9. Keep sound and music clips brief.
10. Always practice the presentation by projecting it to check projection quality.

Slides—Photographic or Digital

Millions of projector and photographic slides used in the presentation world can be projected directly from a laptop using PowerPoint or other presentation software. Whether the slides are photographic or digital—the guidelines are the same.

Advantages of Using Slides

As a guideline, use slides when:

◆ **Your presentation is formal**—making slides does not present a technical challenge, especially if you have access to a digital projector and presentation software.

◆ **Your audience is large**—large venues can support large-screen presentations.

◆ **You will be repeating the presentation frequently**— photographic slides can be safely stored in protective pages in three-ring binders or you can store them right in slide carousels, ready to pop into a projector. Digital slide presentations can also be stored electronically on disks or other electronic media. As a best practice, you might want to do both so that you have a backup.

When Not to Use Slides

Since slides, like other visual aids, are not a one-size-fits-all solution, avoid using slides when:

◆ **Your presentation is informal**—why go to the trouble of making slides when a flipchart or quick presentation software solution would be just as effective?

◆ **You want to make changes to the presentation on the fly**—flipcharts and overhead transparencies enable you to make quick changes easily. If you are using traditional slides, revisions can be costly in terms of both time and money.

Videotapes and DVDs

Using informational videotapes and DVDs can be an effective part of a presentation as a means of getting across a concept, providing background information, or simply offering some entertainment or a catalyst for discussion.

Using Videotapes and DVDs

When requesting and checking the presentation site setup, make sure that the proper equipment is available, works, and you know how to use it. Few things are as embarrassing as having to apologize for equipment failures or your lack of expertise.

Depending on the size of the room and the audience, make sure that there are enough monitors throughout the room so that the entire audience can see. Usually a minimum of one 25-inch monitor strategically placed will do the trick. Your presentation will not be a hit if 50 people are craning their necks to see a videotape on a table at the front of the room.

Plan to show only short segments of the video—no more than 10 to 15 minutes each—before stopping the video and discussing the content.

When you purchase a training video or DVD, you automatically have permission to use that video in presentations as you see fit. However, commercial videos/DVDs are not included under this umbrella. If you purchase or rent a popular movie and use it in a presentation without written permission from the film producers, you are possibly violating copyright law, depending on the nature of your use and the organization in which the presentation takes place. Check this out before making a commercial movie part of your presentation.

Advantages of Videotapes and DVDs

As a guideline, use videotapes or DVDs when:

◆ **You want to dramatically illustrate a point**—or you want to entertain as well as inform the audience. These visual aids are particularly effective for demonstrating desired skills and behavior.

When Not to Use Videotapes and DVDs

As is true for any visual aid, proper use always needs to be considered. Do not use videotapes or DVDs when:

◆ **Your time is limited**—videos often stimulate discussion. The content will not be very valuable if you do not have time to discuss it.

◆ **You want to update or change your message**—changes to a video are expensive and can be very tricky.

Handouts

Handouts usually consist of either additional information related to your presentation or are the hard copies of what was presented on a visual such as a flipchart or electronic presentation slides. Handouts are important for a number of reasons:

◆ They reinforce your message as well as all key and supporting points.

◆ They free the audience to listen to the presentation rather than frantically taking notes.

◆ They enable you to provide additional information to participants that you might not be able to cover fully due to time constraints.

◆ They enable your audience to personalize the materials by taking notes, highlighting important information and jotting ideas for key takeaways.

Using Handouts

Just like any other visual aid you use for a presentation, handouts need to look professional. Be careful not to use too many different styles of fonts and proof the pages to ensure that there are no mis-spellings. Staple or paperclip the handouts if they have multiple pages. This will make it easier for you to distribute them and to ensure the audience has received all the pages. If you know that the audience is receiving a three-ring binder to store all of their presentation materials, they will appreciate it if you have already hole-punched your presentation handouts as well.

The number of copies to make is determined by room capacity. At conferences where attendance at a specific session is not pre-registered, presenters should produce a number of handouts that equals room capacity plus 20 percent.

So with copies in hand, when is the best time to distribute the handouts? In general,

- ◆ Presentation handouts are usually provided at the start of the presentation.
- ◆ Keep in mind, however, that if you distribute handouts before the presentation—to encourage note taking, the audience may pay more attention to the handouts or frantically flip through pages to jump ahead to other topics.
- ◆ If you want to "reveal" your presentation as you go and not have the audience know what is ahead, wait to distribute your handouts until the end.
- ◆ Ideally, handouts that you plan to provide at the start of the presentation should already be placed on the tables or chairs where your audience will be seated.
- ◆ If you have handouts regarding additional resources or supplemental information, those are usually distributed at the close of the session.
- ◆ If you do plan to provide handouts at the end of the session, make arrangements for someone to assist you, especially if the audience is large. It's a little distracting to be speaking to the audience, wrapping up the presentation, and delivering handouts all at the same time.

Props

Presenters often overlook props as a visual aid—and only your imagination limits the type of props that you can use.

For example, Roger VanOech, author of *A Whack on the Side of the Head*, brings volunteers up on stage to represent the four sides of the creative person. Each volunteer dons headgear to illustrate the characteristic he or she represents. Even years later, an average audience member reports recalling the four characteristics based on the four "hats."

Another creative presenter took a basketball in one hand and a baseball in the other as he described the differences in weight of two issues he was presenting.

Introducing anything like props into your presentation also takes a little courage. After all, the approach might fly or people might not quite understand the symbolism. Try out your props when doing a run-through of your presentation with friends or colleagues.

Now that we have explored the many options available for enhancing presentations, use Tool 3.1 to check that the visual aids you will be using follow best-practice guidelines.

TOOL 3.1
Visual Aids Assessment

This assessment will help you to determine which visual aids may be most appropriate for your presentation and to verify that the visuals you have planned will enhance, not distract, from your message.

❏ Is the size of the audience and configuration of the room appropriate for the visual aids you have planned? Will everyone be able to easily see the visual aids?

❏ Are handouts necessary either at the beginning or end of the presentation?

❏ Do the visual aids you have planned match your needs?
   ◆ Are they easily transported?
   ◆ Can they be reused if you need to give the same presentation several times?
   ◆ Can they be easily modified?

❏ What is your comfort level with using technology during the presentation? Will you have adequate time to practice using the technology and rehearse your presentation?

❏ How much time do you have to create all of the visual aids you have planned for the presentation?

❏ Is your handwriting legible or do you need to have the visual aids professionally produced? Do you have a sufficient budget for all of the visual aids planned?

❏ Have you illustrated one point per visual?

❏ Are you using no more than three visual aides every five to six minutes?

❏ Do the visual aids complement what you plan to say—not duplicate exactly what you will say?

❏ Should certain visual aids be displayed for quick reference during the entire presentation (e.g., flipcharts or visuals of a process flow, and so on)?

❏ Is the design of visual aids consistent throughout the presentation (e.g., color scheme, type face, horizontal or vertical orientation, placement of headings, consistent use of bulleted or numbered lists)?

❏ Are the visual aids easy to read?
   ◆ From the back of the room (use black or blue type)?
   ◆ When using different colors to highlight different information (e.g., red can be difficult to see at a distance and colorblind participants may not be able to see a difference between red and green text)?

❏ Are the key points displayed consistently at the beginning and end of the presentation to help orient the audience to your message?

continued on next page

Tool 3.1, continued

❑ Are your visual aids numbered or referenced appropriately in your notes regarding when they should appear during the presentation?

❑ Do you have a flipchart or overhead transparency available in case you need to create visual aids on the fly to help clarify or illustrate your points?

❑ If you are using slides, transparencies, or flipcharts, did you adhere to the rule of no more than six lines per page and no more than six words per line?

❑ Do any visual aids depict an unfamiliar object? If so, how will you help the audience understand its size, shape, and context to the presentation?

❑ Have you checked the spelling of all visual aids?

NOTES

_____
_____
_____
_____
_____
_____
_____
_____
_____
_____
_____
_____
_____
_____
_____
_____
_____
_____
_____
_____
_____
_____
_____
_____
_____
_____

Make It Memorable— Add Pizzazz to the Presentation

STEP **4**

One of the key steps to creating and delivering a successful presentation is to add elements of surprise and interest that engage the audience at the start of the presentation and maintain that level of interest throughout the presentation. Various techniques help you to do just that, including openers and icebreakers, acquainters, stories, humor, analogies, anecdotes, metaphors, tables, graphs, energizers, games, demonstrations, and brainstorming techniques.

Keep in mind that every presentation needs to have the five standard components discussed in chapter 2. Use the techniques described in this chapter to cleverly lead your audience through an engaging and memorable presentation.

Attention-Grabbing Openers and Icebreakers

How often have you attended a presentation that quickly fell flat after the housekeeping details were discussed? Icebreakers and openers immediately get people involved, foster interaction, stimulate creative thinking, challenge basic assumptions, illustrate new concepts, and introduce specific material.

Remember, effective openings and icebreakers should accomplish three things:

- ◆ grab the audience's attention
- ◆ express the main point of the presentation
- ◆ express the benefit and explain what the audience can expect to get out of the presentation.

Two categories of icebreakers include openers and warm-ups, and "getting acquainted." Each of these serves a different purpose.

- ◆ **Openers and Warm-Ups**—these icebreakers warm up a group by stimulating, challenging, and motivating the audience. They can be used to begin a session, start a discussion, prime the group after a break, ready the audience for new material, or shift the topic focus.
- ◆ **Getting Acquainted**—these icebreakers serve two functions: they establish nonthreatening introductory contacts, and they increase participants' familiarity with one another and usually are not tied to the presentation content directly.

Openers

Openers differ from acquainters in that they introduce or tie in to the topic of the presentation. They are intended to set the stage, avoid abrupt starts, and generally make participants comfortable with the program they are about to experience. Openers can energize groups after coffee breaks or lunch and may be used to begin a session on subsequent days of a program.

How to Use Openers

This section provides some ideas for openers and how they can be used in presentations. You may need to personalize these ideas so that they are applicable to your presentation. Sometimes canned icebreakers or openers just don't fit the presentation need, and you may have to create your own. The key principle to remember in designing your own icebreakers is to make them relevant to the presentation content.

- **For small-groups presentations**—and depending on the amount of time you have for the presentation—ask participants to introduce themselves.

- **For large-group presentations**, have audience members pair up with someone they do not know who is seated nearby. Allow a few minutes for the pairs to interview each other about who they are, where they are from, and what they hope to get out of the session.

- **For tough audiences**—ask participants a question to get them thinking. For example, have them rate their personal productivity on a scale of 1–10, with 10 being perfect. (The answers will typically range from 6–8). Then ask them "What is keeping you from being at a higher number?" Allow them several minutes to think this through. Finally, ask them, "What is it costing to stay at the lower number?" As they answer, arms tend to unfold and ears perk up as the presenter explains how the session will address this issue.

Acquainters

Acquainters may have no relation to the topic of the presentation. They are designed to put participants at ease and relieve the initial anxiety that comes with any new beginning.

How to Use Acquainters
Personalize these acquainters to apply to your presentations. For example, in the activity called **Fancy Sayings**, to "translate" written communications, project the following on a screen and have them "decode" the meaning:

- A feathered vertebrate enclosed in the grasping organ has an estimated worth that is higher than a duo encapsulated in the branched shrub. (A bird in the hand is worth two in the bush.)

◆ It is sufficiently more tolerable to bestow upon than to come into possession. (It is better to give than to receive.)

◆ The medium of exchange is the origin or source of the mount of sorrow, distress, and calamity. (Money is the root of all evil.)

◆ A monetary unit equal to 1/100 of a pound that is stored aside is a monetary unit equal to 1/100 of a pound that is brought in by way of returns. (A penny saved is a penny earned.)

The Power of Storytelling

Storytelling is an interesting, proven, and inexpensive way to communicate memorable messages. People like to hear stories, and they tend to repeat them. In business, as well as other settings, storytelling works as a useful technique to

◆ capture an audience's attention
◆ send a message the audience will remember
◆ establish rapport
◆ build credibility
◆ build cohesion.

We all know presenters and leaders who seem to have an innate ability to tell stories. They are able to pull out an appropriate tale with a poignant message, just right for the situation or audience at hand. But however magical good storytelling can appear, it is an art (and a science) that you can learn and use to communicate key messages.

So how can you harness this art of storytelling? Begin by reflecting on your past experiences, understanding the meanings inherent in them, and using those stories deliberately to send key messages in a variety of contexts and audiences. In particular, you should

1. identify the message you want to send
2. find stories to reinforce your message
3. develop stories
4. deliver your stories.

Step 1: Identify the Message You Want to Send

The first step in the strategic-storytelling process is to identify the message you want to send. A good question to ask yourself is, "What is the key message(s) that I want the audience to remember?" Then work to identify and develop stories that reinforce the message. This approach enables you to personalize the message in an intimate and authentic way at the same time.

Step 2: Find Stories to Reinforce Your Message

The appropriate stories to select and tell will depend on the message you want to send. When selecting a story to wrap around the message, it is best to pick one that is relevant to your audience's experience and background. Stories that you can tell in the first person—meaning that you are also a character—work best.

When identifying what makes a good story, think about the kinds of stories you like to hear. The following are elements of a good story:

♦ **The story has a point**—the story has a clear message that the audience can infer from the plot, but is not so moralistic or obvious that it overwhelms the plot.

♦ **The theme is relevant**—the story enables your audience to resonate with your point and recall their own relevant stories and experiences.

♦ **The story is interesting**—the story has a strong plot, colorful content, and interesting characters.

- ◆ **The content is real**—the characters, locations, and settings have names and are well described.
- ◆ **The story is authentic**—it contains truthful elements around which the teller has a personal commitment.

Good storytellers have good stories because they listen for them and recognize when they find themselves in one. Great stories might come from your own personal and professional experiences, the experiences of your colleagues, or involve organizations relevant to your presentation.

Step 3: Develop Stories

Once you have a collection of stories to consider, determine which will be most useful for transmitting each key point or message. Stories will not always emerge intact with a strong message, vivid plot, and enthralling characters. Most stories will require some embellishment and practice to make them memorable and meaningful.

It is okay to embellish your story to achieve maximum impact.

When thinking through story development, remember a good story has a beginning and an end. Consider the best point in time to begin your story, and develop an engaging start to draw the audience in. Think about the pinnacle moments in the story, and how you can leverage them for maximum impact. And of course, your story should have a natural and clear ending. The best way to continue developing your story is to tell it a few times and ask for feedback from a friendly critic on how you can improve the story.

Step 4: Deliver Your Stories

Perhaps the most important characteristic of an effective storyteller is the ability to remain authentic—meaning, staying true to your own stories and maintaining the integrity of stories you select to retell. This means sharing truthful and relevant facts and detail.

Authenticity also shows up on your face. When you are truly engaged in the story, your audience can tell by your facial expressions and body language. By sharing the emotion you feel in the telling of the story, you help the audience resonate with you and your message.

Another key element in delivery is how you "spin" the story. Putting a positive spin on a story helps to engage the audience and ensures the message is productive. A story does not need to be happy to be positive; you can tell sad or tragic stories in a positive light.

For example, one presenter told the following story:

> I was dining with relatives in a fine restaurant, when a policeman appeared and informed me that my daughter had been thrown from a Jeep. She was hurt, but would be okay. I spent a sleepless weekend caring for my daughter and managing the many relatives who were around to help. When the phone rang with an urgent business problem, I unleashed my frustration in an angry and inappropriate way to the employee who had made the business mistake.

So far, this story sounds far from positive. However, the "spin" this presenter put on the story was one of self-reflection and growth. His story ended:

> I realize now the negative impact that I must have had on that employee. No matter what is going on at home, it is important to separate emotions enough to consider the effect you are having on others. This guy will probably never forget what I said to him and how I said it,

and yet, what he heard at that moment had more to do with me than him.

His tragic story had a positive spin. The presenter, turned story-teller, came across as authentic, and compassionate, and the audience was left with a memorable message.

Examples and stories from your own experiences help to illustrate and reinforce your current point. Practice telling stories so that you are prepared to emphasize the points that are most illustrative. You can even leave out part of it and then tell the rest of the story later, or you can ask the audience, "What do you think happened next?"

Avoid "Winging It"

Winging it with examples and stories doesn't work. You can get off schedule in a big way. If you select a story to tell on the spot, you might be stealing your thunder for a later content point. You might get to the end and discover that the main point isn't really relevant to the content at hand. Some presenters even get to the end of a spur-of-the-moment story and realize that not only does it not make a point, but also that the punch line is offensive. Think through your telling of examples and stories.

Do not throw in a story without planning it first. You can get lost and go nowhere.

Using Humor Effectively

Humor and laughter help improve, maintain, and enhance participant interest. Camaraderie begins to develop when the presenter and participants share a pun, story, or other common experience. Humor fosters a "team" atmosphere and promotes a positive experience.

- Use topic-related cartoons, stories, puns, and anecdotes to emphasize and reinforce points throughout your presentation.
- Maintain a file of humorous stories, pictures, drawings, and related materials.
- The humorous item must be relevant to the presentation and content at hand. Telling a story or joke just for fun takes the presentation off track.
- Avoid humor that might offend or alienate participants. Make sure your joke or story is clean. Perhaps this cautionary note seems obvious, but for some presenters, it isn't. Using even mild curse words is offensive to some members of the audience and makes you look unprofessional. Don't think that if your audience swears, you can too. Part of your role is to model professional behavior.
- Practice telling stories *before* the presentation so that you can practice what to emphasize and exaggerate, and so you don't forget the punch line.
- Laugh *with* not *at* others.
- Laugh at yourself, particularly when a story or pun flops. This puts the audience at ease and indicates that you are comfortable with the group and self-confident about your presentation.
- Don't use jokes that stereotype racial groups, age groups, ethnic groups, the sexes, or other characteristics of people that are not related to the presentation. This includes your own group!
- Use humor to be inclusive—not exclusive. All audience members might not get the joke, for example, if you make a reference to a current event or a current movie. Be prepared to explain it or don't use the reference at all. One of the worst things a presenter can do is to exclude some members of the audience.

If telling stories and humor isn't your long suit—it is perfectly acceptable not to do it. Take advantage of how you prefer to personalize your presentation with your own talents.

S T E P POINTER

Humor in Icebreakers

Humor is a right-brain, creative activity that helps presenters to emphasize or reinforce the key and supporting points of a presentation. Humor provides a completely different perspective for an icebreaker. It can help relax the audience in tension-producing situations and can make a marginally interesting activity or subject more interesting, even exciting.

Are you a juggler, amateur magician, a poet, a songwriter? The list goes on with different ways that your can personalize your presentation to help convey the key or supporting points.

Building the Body with Text, Tables, and Graphs

Chapter 3 provided guidelines for working with various visual aids. Whether you use visual aids to show what something looks like, or you choose text or other visuals to show how to do something, to clarify relationships, or to show how something is organized, four rules are paramount:

- ◆ make it big
- ◆ keep it simple
- ◆ make it clear
- ◆ be consistent.

Experienced presenters know that selecting the right way to communicate and deliver information is as important as what you say. That's where text, such as metaphors, analogies, and anecdotes not only engage audiences but they help you to convey information more clearly.

When you need to discuss numbers and data to communicate relationships and trends, graphs or tables help your audience to see the information organized in a specific way to clearly communicate the trend or relationship that you are describing. Let's look at different ways that text, tables, and graphs can add pizzazz to a presentation.

Guidelines for Visuals

It's easy to overestimate how big text and graphic images will be when projected onto a screen. A general rule is that if the text or image looks big enough to be the right size, it's probably too small—make your text and images so large that you think they must be too big. There are a few ways to help you gauge the size and readability of your visuals:

◆ To determine the size of the projected image in relation to the viewing distance, use the "6W" formula: one foot of the screen width is required for each six feet of viewing distance from the screen.

◆ Measure in inches the width of the art or text to be projected. Divide by two. Hold the graphic that many feet away from a friendly critic and ask him or her to read or describe the image.

◆ If the text of your visual appears too crowded when you write it with a felt marker on an 8.5 × 11 inch size paper, it's too long. For text visuals, use a large font, at least 36 or 48 point, and use a maximum of six words per line, six lines per visual.

◆ Fit your image onto a 4 × 6 inch index card, place it on the floor, and look down at it. If you can read it, the size is probably about right.

◆ If you're designing the image on a computer, move 6 feet away from the screen. Can you read it? If not, it's too small.

If the visual depicts an unfamiliar object, show it in comparison to a familiar object so that your audience understands its size and shape. If you are showing photographs or drawings of equipment and materials that the audience will be using, show them from the point of view of the person using them on the job.

POINTER

Make your visuals big. People do not want to struggle to see them.

Text

If your text is too long or complicated, your audience probably will not get the point. And if your graphics are too elaborate, the audience is likely to be distracted, or you may even trigger some responses disruptive to your presentation (for example, collective awe, hilarity, sidetracked conversations, and so on).

For text visuals, use an easy-to-read serif (for example, Bookman, Palatino, Times) or san serif (for example, Helvetica, Avant Garde) typeface. A mix of upper and lower case letters is easiest to read—don't use all caps or script. Keep graphic visuals uncluttered—don't be afraid of white space. Heavy grid lines, excessive tick marks, and other superfluous information will confuse your audience. Use only the data that you need to get your message across.

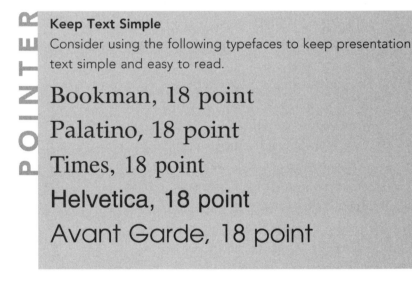

Keep Text Simple
Consider using the following typefaces to keep presentation text simple and easy to read.

Bookman, 18 point

Palatino, 18 point

Times, 18 point

Helvetica, 18 point

Avant Garde, 18 point

When displaying text on slides, remember the guideline of six lines per slide and no more than six words per line. Text that is flush left with ragged-right justification is easiest on the eyes. For emphasis, use color, boldface, or larger type—make sure to use it consistently and sparingly. Use bullets for nonsequential items;

for sequential items use Arabic numerals, not letters or Roman numerals. Be sure to proofread all visuals for spelling, grammar, and meaning.

Quotations

Quotations from other sources, strategically placed in the beginning, middle, or end of your presentation, often have the effect of stimulating people's thinking. Before you use a quote, though, be sure of its authenticity—especially if you found it online—and its relevance to the subject matter. When you use a quote, always give attribution to the appropriate source.

Metaphors

Metaphors, as well as analogies and anecdotes, are thought-provoking forms of speech that open people's minds to think differently about a subject or issue. According to *Webster's Eleventh New Collegiate Dictionary* (Merriam-Webster, 2005), a metaphor is a "figure of speech in which a word or phrase literally denoting one kind of object or idea is used in place of another to suggest a likeness or analogy between them."

One presenter speaking at a career development seminar used the New York marathon as a metaphor for the effort involving in searching for a new job. As he planted a picture in the minds of his audience of the daunting task of running the marathon, he explained that conducting a job search was similar because those who are successful in completing the journey in the shortest time are always the ones who spent the most time preparing themselves.

Analogies

An analogy, according to *Webster's*, is a "resemblance in some particulars between things otherwise unlike." Analogies, like metaphors, often help paint a picture in people's minds that help people to "see" concepts or ideas more clearly. One presenter, wanting to lay the foundation for introducing a new financial reporting system, used this analogy: "Trying to reconcile our old monthly financial reports was like putting together a jigsaw puzzle only to find some of the pieces missing." Nodding their heads in agreement, the listeners became eager, wanting to learn more about this new, less frustrating system.

Tables

Consider using a table when you need to provide data in a precise form. Be prepared to discuss the statistical assessment of the data and its implication, and provide sources, if necessary. Be sure to proofread the table and ensure the accuracy of the numbers and calculations.

Graphs

Graphs are an effective way to present data, show trends, and demonstrate relationships. However, some graphs are more effective at accomplishing these goals than others. In general:

- ◆ **Bar graphs**—show relationships between two or more variables at one time or at several points in time. Improve readability of a bar chart by making the bars wider than the spaces between them. Don't make graphs too complicated—readability and the ability to understand the information are key to making the graph of value to the audience. As a general guideline, the audience should be able to read and understand the graph in fewer than 30 seconds.
- ◆ **Line graphs**—show a progression of changes over time. Be sure to label axes, data lines, and data points clearly. Be careful not to exaggerate the data points by changing the scale (for example, 0–100 or 1–50) or gridlines in the background to make something look more significant than it really is. Tick marks often clutter a graph—so use them sparingly and only if they add clarity for the audience. Gridlines or other graph elements that do not add clarity should be omitted.
- ◆ **Pie charts**—show the relationships between the parts of a unit at a given moment. Include only essential information in pie charts and avoid having more than six wedges of

the pie. Smaller pie slices can always be lumped into an "other" category.

Energizers and Games

It's a rainy day after lunch and the audience is running out of gas. Their eyelids are drooping and you're trying to figure out how to bring oxygen to their brains and breathe life back into the presentation.

The training industry has long touted studies indicating that adults are likely to forget 50 percent of a presentation's content when delivered through passive means (that is, lectures with little interaction). Another study indicated that approximately half of one day's information may be lost during the ensuing 24 hours. So if you want your presentation to engage the audience and have longer-lasting effects, energizers and games may be just the ticket.

POINTER Getting the audience physically involved keeps them engaged and helps them remember your message.

Energizers

Energizers are used when the participants appear overly stressed or when the group is "flat." For example, if the presentation is getting bogged down with a heavy topic or discussion, you can speed up the pace by introducing an energizer. When participants feel more relaxed, they will be receptive to a more open dialogue about the information or issues to be introduced. Energizers are also great to use if the audience has been sitting for quite some time; getting them up and a little more active will raise the energy in the room and re-engage them in the presentation content. Energizers can:

◆ Change the pace of the presentation
◆ Increase audience participation and the energy level of the group
◆ Create transitions from one topic to another.

Some examples of energizes include

◆ Turn to the person next to you and practice or discuss an item assigned by the presenter (for example, using the "five why" technique to uncover business needs).

◆ Teams race to complete an assignment based on the presentation content (for example, brainstorm three ways to reduce the monthly expenses in your department by 5 percent and still achieve the organizational objectives).

◆ Write one thing that they learned during the presentation that they plan to implement immediately back on the job.

◆ Participants—led by you—stretch, relax, do head rolls, and take deep breaths to relax and reinvigorate themselves.

Games and Brainteasers

Games and brainteasers are effective warm-ups. Games can function as introductions to problem solving, competition, team building, and consensus-seeking activities, while brainteasers reduce information overload when the material being presented becomes too cumbersome or draining.

Games can have a significant impact on your audience in helping them to comprehend the presentation content on several levels. For example, games can be used to identify, examine, critique, or discuss a problem; to develop skills such as empathetic listening, communication, problem solving, decision making, or management; or to start up, conclude, or refresh a problem.

How to Use Games

◆ **Organize the activity**—by establishing clear and specific objectives. You can proceed down a logical path only if you know where you are going.

◆ **Design resource materials**—to fit the content and compile a list of materials for every phase of the game: instructions, forms, information sheets, background reading, diagrams, charts, and props.

- ◆ **Plan in sequence**—each phase of an activity should enhance the next.
- ◆ **Build in ways to gather data**—by including listeners, observers, questionnaires, assigning one person to "report" back on a group's findings, or having a group create a flipchart on their information.

When conducting games, be sure to clarify expectations at the beginning of the presentation section to ensure that the participants understand the objectives and game rules. Make a contract with the group, agreeing on expectations, roles, responsibilities, and norms. Post a list of participant expectations so that the audience can refer to them during the game to ensure they are meeting your expectations.

Intervene only when necessary; encourage participants to be assertive and not to rely on you to defend or protect them. Give support and be willing to accept it from the group. Ask for feedback and respond to it.

The Don'ts of Game Presentation

Guard against these common mistakes when conducting games as part of your presentation:

- ◆ Do not use excessively difficult or threatening games.
- ◆ Do not distance yourself from presentation participants.
- ◆ Do not use the same techniques repeatedly.
- ◆ Do not change the game to appease a few people in the group.
- ◆ Do not become more concerned with the game than the purpose of the game to support the presentation goals.

Brainstorming

In brainstorming, the idea is to come up with as many ideas as possible and then whittle them down to a couple that seem the most promising. Brainstorming promotes collaborative problem solving by getting the audience or small groups to focus on creating and expanding a list of possibilities.

The number of people who can participate has no limit, but presenters often break larger audiences into subgroups of four to five participants to create and expand a list of possible ideas or solutions. In brainstorming, record and recognize all ideas, no matter how outlandish. Postpone evaluation of ideas put forward until the next step in the process.

How to Use Brainstorming

Brainstorming is an excellent way to engage the audience by posing a problem for which you want them to develop solutions or to generate a list of ideas related to a specific topic. When facilitating brainstorming as part of your presentation, use these steps:

1. Assign a question or get the groups to agree on a central question related to the presentation content.
2. Each participant in the group needs to suggest at least one idea or solution to the question posed.
3. Have one person in each group capture all ideas generated—no matter how outlandish. Postpone evaluation of ideas put forward until the next step in the process.
4. Call time.
5. Depending on the purpose of the brainstorming session, have the groups either go back and select the top five ideas to develop further and refine or go back and generate ideas for each solution posed.
6. Have the groups review the completed list for clarity, duplication, and to make their final recommendations.

Demonstrations

Demonstrations typically involve someone showing the participants the process of modeling a procedure. Some techniques for types of demonstrations include

- ◆ **Role play**—Use role play between the presenter and a helper or audience member to demonstrate a technique or make a point, followed with discussion.
- ◆ **Coaching**—Use coaching to provide guidance and feedback, for example, if participants are working in pairs on communication, listening, or other skill practice.

To make your presentation more memorable use Worksheet 4.1 to help you decide which of these attention-getting techniques will best suit your needs.

WORKSHEET 4.1

Make-Your-Presentation-Memorable Checklist

This checklist will help you assess and plan additional elements to add to your presentation that help to create surprise and interest to engage your audience at the start of the presentation, and to maintain that level of interest throughout your speech. Review the techniques outlined in the table below to plan which items are most appropriate to meet the needs of your presentation.

Technique	Purpose	Include?	How can I implement this technique in the presentation?
Openers & Warm-Ups	To stimulate, motivate, and challenge the group at the start of the presentation	☐	
Acquainters	To increase participant familiarity with one another	☐	
Storytelling	To capture the audience's attention, convey a message the audience will remember, establish rapport, build credibility, and build cohesion	☐	

S T E P
4

	Purpose	
Humor	To improve, maintain, and enhance audience interest, build camaraderie, or foster a team atmosphere to promote a positive experience	☐
Quotations	To stimulate thinking in the beginning, middle, or end of your presentation	☐
Metaphors	To introduce a thought-provoking form of speech that helps people to think differently about a subject or issue	☐
Analogy	To paint a picture in the audience members' minds to help them see concepts or ideas more clearly	☐
Tables	To display data in a specific format to help the audience to readily understand a series of numbers, calculations, and their relationship	☐

Graphs	To present data, show trends, and demonstrate relationships	☐
Energizers	To help relax the audience when they appear overly stressed or increase the energy when the group appears "flat"	☐
Games	To serve as warm-ups or introductions to problem solving, competition, team building, and consensus-seeking activities	☐
Brainteasers	To reduce information overload when the material being presented becomes too cumbersome or draining	☐
Brainstorming	To generate as many ideas as possible and then whittle them down to a couple that seem the most promising	☐
Demonstrations	To show the participants a process by modeling a procedure	☐

STEP

4

NOTES

_____

_____

_____

_____

_____

_____

_____

_____

_____

_____

_____

_____

_____

_____

_____

_____

_____

_____

_____

_____

_____

_____

_____

_____

Make Sure the Venue and Environment Work in Your Favor

It's a common scenario: the presentation room is too hot, the lights are too dim, and the coffee is tepid. The speaker is miles away, the slide projector does not focus, and the other attendees are grumbling to one another in small groups about "a waste of time."

This chapter focuses on ways you can make sure the physical environment of your presentation site helps you to deliver a successful presentation. Keep in mind that today's meeting rooms might be very high tech—yet technology should be used only to augment and not become the primary focus of the presentation.

Staging the Environment

The physical environment can have a major impact on the success of any presentation. No matter how well designed the presentation, regardless of how talented and entertaining you are as a presenter, a good session in a poor environment might add up to a waste of time and money for everyone involved.

When selecting a room be sure that the physical setting matches the presentation goals. Presentations can take place in an amazing range of rooms including theaters, storage rooms, classrooms, restaurants, and so on. Given the inevitable limitations that come along with the type of room assigned for your presentation, you must express your wants and needs, if you have a say in where and when you give your presentation. When you are asked what you want and need—never say (or think), "Don't worry about me, any place is fine." Take advantage of the opportunity to have control over the room logistics and the ability to create a comfortable atmosphere and to meet your presentation needs.

Setting Up the Room

The single most important factor that determines the success of any presentation is the seating. Placement of chairs—and possibly tables—can contribute immensely to accomplishing the presentation objectives.

POINTER

The one thing that determines the success of a presentation is the seating.

Determining where people will sit can influence the level of participation. Some seating arrangements make it difficult—if not impossible—to interrupt a speaker. Other arrangements encourage participation of the entire group. So depending on how much you want to control the group, or get their direct involvement, use one of the seating arrangements described in this section.

There is no single way to set up a room for a presentation. Because some setups work better for certain kinds of presentations, be sure to state your preferences. Descriptions of each type of room setup follow. Table 5.1 lists the most common room setups, as well as when to use each type.

Rounds

Some also refer to this configuration as pods. Actually, the term *rounds* connotes the shape of the table used—when in reality the

TABLE 5.1

Room Setup Matrix

Style	When to Use	When Not to Use	Alternatives
Rounds	◆ Larger groups ◆ Work in teams ◆ Small-group interaction ◆ When using audiovisuals	◆ Room too small ◆ Group less than 15	◆ Classroom ◆ Chevron
Classroom	◆ Any size group depending on room size ◆ When using audiovisuals ◆ When focus is on the presenter	◆ You want group interaction ◆ Room dimensions are too long or wide	◆ Chevron ◆ Rounds ◆ U-shape
U-Shape	◆ Smaller group size ◆ Open environment ◆ When using audiovisuals	◆ Small room ◆ Large group ◆ Work in teams	◆ Classroom ◆ Chevron ◆ Conference
Chevron	◆ Large groups ◆ For presenters who like to move ◆ When using visuals	◆ When a warm, personal atmosphere is needed	◆ U-shape ◆ Rounds ◆ Classroom
Conference	◆ Small group ◆ Group discussion ◆ Formal and intimate	◆ Room to spread out ◆ Using audiovisuals that require room ◆ Presenter movement	◆ Classroom ◆ U-shape
Theater	◆ Large group ◆ Focus on presenter ◆ When using audiovisuals	◆ Establish intimate environment ◆ Small group ◆ Group interaction	◆ Rounds ◆ Classroom ◆ Chevron

STEP 5

table shape might really be square or rectangular. In this configuration, the presenter and any audiovisual equipment are usually at the front of the room. Although the number of people at each table will vary, table seating usually averages between four and 10 people, depending on the number of tables and the size of the audience. Rounds work well for an audience of at least 15 people, especially when you want them to work in small groups on complete an activity or game. This setup creates a friendly environment with the flexibility to choose the best audiovisuals to support your presentation.

Setting up rounds requires a room large enough to allow ample space between the tables without chairs brushing up next to each other. The biggest challenge of using this setup is that some participants may need to crane their necks to see the presenter or audiovisuals based on the position of their chairs.

Classroom Style

This is similar to traditional school-classroom seating with rows of desks or tables and chairs all facing the presenter, who is standing in front. This type of arrangement usually creates a formal atmosphere with all eyes on the presenter; it does not allow for a great deal of movement or interaction among participants.

Most participants will be able to easily see both high- and low-tech visual aids, including flipcharts, whiteboards, and presentation software or slides. However, if the room is very long or very wide, some audience members may feel like they are in the remote recesses of the room and may have difficulty seeing any visuals.

U-Shaped Configuration

This room configuration is often popular for a workshop type of a setting in which all participants can see one another and the presenter has plenty of room to walk around. This setup is particularly useful when you want to have groups of two or three people talk or work together.

This setup works best for groups of 12 to 24 people if the room is large enough. If the group is too big or too small, then the purpose of this room setup is defeated. Be careful not to cram too many tables and chairs into a room that is too small. This will make it difficult for participants to walk around the outside of the table, and to leave the room when needed.

Chevron

This arrangement combines the best features of the classroom and rounds arrangements. Like the classroom setup, rows of tables are placed at an angle and positioned behind each other. This forms the letter "V" with a main aisle in the middle. Like the rounds setup, it makes for easy pairing of groups or teams already set at the different tables.

This setup offers two main benefits. It can accommodate large groups and since the tables are angled, participants can easily maneuver and walk around the room. This setup also enables the presenter to easily walk down the main aisle and to make a variety of visual aids visible to the audience.

One disadvantage is that the participants in the back of the room, even with the tables angled, might have difficulty seeing some of the visuals if the group is large. This type of setup also does not create a very warm or intimate setup since most of the participants are looking at the back of the people in front of them.

Conference Style

This style usually involves the audience sitting in chairs around a large conference table. The presenter can take a seat at the table, either at the head for a stronger presence, or at any chair for a more informal effect. This type of arrangement works well for both formal and informal presentations in which the audience is relatively small, depending on the size of the room.

This is an ideal setup if your intent is to add some importance to the presentation (boardroom) by bringing people into a setting that is intimate and conducive to a personal presentation and discussion. Keep in mind that some people might be a bit confined if they cannot walk around the table. Also, the conference style is not as conducive to team or group activity as rounds or other setups.

Theater

Theater (sometimes called auditorium) usually refers to seating in a large room with fixed seats that cannot be moved. This arrangement works well for large groups where the focus is on the presenter and not on audience interaction. This venue also enables

Avoiding Venue Pitfalls

Every presentation planner has horror stories he or she would rather forget. Everyone who conducts meetings, conferences, or training programs is going to make a few mistakes, but the goal is to get tripped up as little as possible. Here are some suggestions to help keep you out of trouble:

◆ Avoid meeting rooms that are ornately decorated. Sometimes hotels offer rooms with busy, flocked wallpaper, or mirrors and large pictures covering the walls. These can distract participants from the presentation content.

◆ Beware of beautiful views. When difficult subject matter requires concentration, using a room with a panoramic view can be quite counterproductive. It is a lot more fun to stare out the window than to focus on figures covering charts and graphs.

◆ Avoid holding presentations in basement rooms where participants might feel trapped.

◆ Do not conduct a presentation in a long, narrow room if a lot of participant movement is required.

◆ If you are presenting to C-level executives of profit-making organizations, choose upscale facilities. In general, hold sessions in rooms that have an environment similar to the workplace.

the presenter a large variety of audiovisual options that all audience members can see easily. Although theater style is usually associated with a morel formal presentation, if the presenter has a wireless microphone, the environment can be informal since the presenter is free to move around the room and interact with the audience.

This room setup is not ideal if you want a warm, intimate environment. If you have a small audience and are booked in a large theater-style room, ask the participants to move closer to the front. One disadvantage of this setup is that it precludes most audience members from actively taking notes unless the seats are equipped with a folding desktop surface.

Other Room Elements to Consider

Screens

Another way to check the adequacy of a room's dimensions is to judge all distances from the width of the screen to be used for visual presentations. Follow these guidelines:

- ◆ The distance from the screen to the last row of seats should not exceed six screen-widths.
- ◆ The distance to the front row of seats should be at least twice the width of the screen. Participants who are closer than that will experience discomfort and fatigue.
- ◆ The proper width of the viewing area is three screen-widths. No one should be more than one screen-width to the left or right of the screen.
- ◆ Ceiling height is important. The room's ceiling should be high enough—a minimum of nine feet—to permit people seated in the last row to see the bottom of the screen by looking over, not around, the heads of those in front of them.
- ◆ Try to use screens that recede into the ceiling and that automatically raise and lower.

Lecterns and Tables

A lectern is a small desk that usually sits on a podium or table on which you can rest your presentation notes. Presenters often speak from behind a lectern when making a formal presentation. Aside from a place to rest your notes, lecterns often act like a security blanket for less-experienced presenters who want to be anchored to one place yet still appear experienced. The trick to pulling this off is to avoid placing a death grip on the lectern, so your knuckles don't turn white.

You might want to consider asking for an appropriately sized table to spread out notes, transparencies, handouts, props, or other presentation materials. If needed, also arrange to have extra tables set up for participant handouts, books, and so on.

Peripheral Facilities

When making arrangements for the meeting room, you should understand the communication requirements of those involved in the meeting. For example, if your presentation is part of a larger program, find out if participants are expected to take calls and check messages only during breaks. To facilitate this, find out if the site has

- ◆ a contact available to take incoming messages
- ◆ a message board in a central location to receive messages, if so, ask participants to check the board during each break
- ◆ a phone line into the presentation room (if one is installed, have it disconnected).

Planning for the Audience's Comfort

Temperature

Because room temperatures can vary wildly, try to ensure that you and your audience will be comfortable. Prior to the presentation be sure that you find out how to control the presentation room's temperature. For example, can you adjust it yourself within the room or do you need to call someone within the building or at a remote location to request a temperature change? Here are some guidelines to consider:

- Set the thermostat for a comfortable temperature, depending on the season, size of the room, and the audience.
- It's probably best if the room is a little cool at the start of the presentation since the room will probably heat up as more people join the session and because some audiovisual equipment tends to throw off quite a bit of heat.
- Keep the room somewhat cooler if the audience is likely to be wearing business suits, which are often made of wool.
- For a daytime presentation in a room with windows, consider the effect of sunlight on the room temperature. Adjust the curtains or blinds—and perhaps the thermostat—accordingly.

Lighting

Lighting is an important factor in creating a comfortable environment for the audience. Not only does it affect the mood of the participants (after lunch is prime sleepy time), but it is also a key factor in how well the audience can see your visual aids and their ability to take notes.

Just as you need to know how to adjust the room temperature, you have to be able to work the lights. Be sure that you know how to dim and change the lighting. The lighting guidelines include

- Find out what lighting operations are available in the presentation site either by asking the sponsor or by visiting the site prior to presentation day.
- Locate the lighting controls for all lights in the room and practice using the dimmer and slide switches.

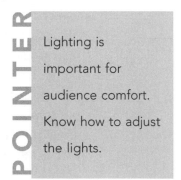

POINTER

Lighting is important for audience comfort. Know how to adjust the lights.

◆ Determine what settings you plan to use during various segments of your presentation. For example, if you are going to go through introductions or an opening activity, turn the lights up bright. Dim the lights when appropriate to enable the audience to see the visual aids with ease.

◆ If you cannot access the lighting controls easily during your presentation, arrange to have someone sit by the controls to make the changes for you. You will need to explain the lighting settings that you want and when they should change during the presentation.

Noise Level

The noise level outside your room can affect your presentation—especially if you're located in a hotel or a noisy conference center. If you are in a room separated from other rooms by a partition or near the kitchen entrance, check the noise level. If the noise is unacceptable, raise your concerns with the sponsor or the facility contact to address the issue.

Food and Breaks

It's not unusual for continental breakfast items or snacks to be readily available in your presentation room or immediately outside the door. In fact, you might even be asked to conduct a presentation over lunch or at a dinner meeting. Since food service can affect your presentation, and if you have any say in the matter, consider the following:

◆ Get to know the people who are handling the food service, and be clear about your expectations regarding the kinds of food that will be served, and when, how, and where the food will be set up.

◆ Opt for lighter, nutritious fare such as fruit or pasta salads, and small sandwiches. Heavier food tends to make people drowsy, especially right after lunch or in the late afternoon. Arrange for plenty of bottled water and juices as alternatives to sodas. Also be sure to have both decaffeinated and caffeinated coffee and tea.

◆ If possible, ask for the food service to be set up in advance so that it does not interfere with your presentation. If this is not possible, arrange for the food to be placed outside the presentation room to minimize the noise and disturbance.

Using Technology Strategically

Audiovisual Setup

Chances are you'll be using at least one audiovisual to support your presentation. Although visuals can really enhance and clarify your presentation content, they can also turn your presentation into a disaster if you haven't appropriately planned and specified what you need in the presentation room. Make sure you have accounted for the following prior to your presentation when using visual aids:

◆ Verify that there are enough outlets to accommodate all audiovisual equipment needs. Know the location of each and arrange for any extension cords or power strips.

◆ Tape down or cover any cords or wires that might pose tripping or electrical hazards.

◆ Familiarize yourself with each piece of equipment before the presentation and "cue up" any visuals.

◆ Prepare a contingency plan if any equipment malfunctions such as locating replacement bulbs, batteries, and so on.

◆ Identify the on-site audiovisual contact and how he/she can be reached should you need help.

Microphones

The most important piece of equipment the speaker needs to be familiar with is the microphone. Characteristics of the four types of mike follow

◆ **Fixed mike**—is attached to the lectern. It has the benefits of being in one location and

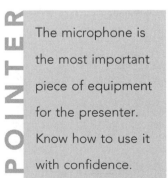

POINTER

The microphone is the most important piece of equipment for the presenter. Know how to use it with confidence.

near a surface that holds speaking notes. However, it often forces the speaker to remain in one place, cutting down the visual impact of the presentation.

◆ **Lavaliere mike**—is attached to the speaker's lapel. It moves around with the speaker. These mikes tend to flatten the range of vocal variety and to favor sound coming directly from above. When the speaker turns his or her head, the lavaliere sometimes misses a few words.

◆ **Hand-held mike**—moves with the speaker and is easy to use for additional voice dynamics. The main disadvantage is that it limits gestures because one hand is holding the mike.

◆ **Wireless mike**—is attached to the speaker's clothing and frees the speaker to broadcast from any spot in the room. Occasionally this type of mike picks up sound from other equipment in the area.

Now that you have considered the presentation environment from all angles, use Tool 5.1 to make sure the room has what you need and nothing goes overlooked.

TOOL 5.1

Presentation Site Checklist

To ensure your meeting site will promote successful presentations, follow these guidelines. Keep in mind that for longer presentations, comfortable chairs are essential.

Location

❏ Is the presentation room located away from high-traffic areas that might lead to interruptions?

❏ Are there signs directing people to presentation sessions, break-out rooms, break areas?

❏ Are telephones available away from the presentation room and in a place that will not disrupt the session?

❏ Is there a system set up to minimize outside interruptions?

❏ Have all telephones been disconnected from inside the presentation room?

❏ Can you easily control the temperature and ventilation in the room?

Room Size and Shape

❏ Is the room the correct size for the type of presentation and activities that you are planning?

❏ Is the room free from any elements that will obstruct the view such as columns?

❏ Is there enough space in the presenter's area for notes, handouts, and other materials that might be used during the presentation?

❏ Is there enough room for audiovisual equipment?

❏ Is there enough clearance between tables and chairs?

❏ Are doorways wide enough for audiovisual equipment and disabled participants to easily pass?

❏ If any breakout rooms are to be used, do they all have the equipment and supplies required, and are they in close proximity to your room?

❏ If you will be leaving the presentation room for a lunch break, can you secure the room to ensure that participant materials, laptops, or other valuable items are safe?

❏ What arrangements do you need to make if the presentation lasts over breaks or multiple days to ensure that cleaning crews do not throw out flipcharts, handouts, or other materials that might be on the walls and tables?

continued on next page

STEP 5

Walls and Ceilings

❒ Can the walls accommodate charts and panels?

❒ Are the walls a neutral color that will not distract the audience?

❒ Are the ceilings high enough to accommodate projection screens?

❒ Do the walls contain enough electrical outlets? If computers are to be used, will antisurge electrical outlets be needed?

❒ Are light switches easily accessible?

❒ Can different parts of the room—for example, at the front of the room near the screen—receive different kinds of lighting?

Noise Control

❒ Is the room too close to the street?

❒ Is the room near an alleyway or loading dock?

❒ Is the room located near building renovation or where heavy machinery is being used?

❒ Are elevators too near the room?

❒ Is a noisy session scheduled for the adjoining room?

❒ Is there a dividing wall that does not shut out noise from the adjacent room?

Furniture

❒ Do chairs have wheels that permit them to be moved without noise?

❒ Depending on the size of the audience, are swivel chairs available?

❒ Do chairs have armrests that allow people to rest their arms at a 90-degree angle?

❒ Are there sufficient whiteboards or flipcharts, as well as markers?

❒ Does the room have tables with modesty panels and separate tables to hold slide or overhead projectors?

❒ Have you checked the audiovisual equipment?

❒ Will the facility have extra light bulbs and extension cords available or do you need to supply them?

Use of Technology

❒ Are there flexible cable outlets for computer hookups?

❒ Are there in-floor jacks?

❒ Are there electrical in-floor outlets at least every eight feet?

STEP 5

NOTES

_____

_____

_____

_____

_____

_____

_____

_____

_____

_____

_____

_____

_____

_____

_____

_____

_____

_____

_____

_____

_____

_____

_____

_____

_____

Stop—Review Basic Communication Techniques

Verbal communication

Nonverbal communication

Using microphones

With solid research finished, a well-crafted presentation in hand, and all of the room logistics scheduled, some presentations can still fail. Why? The presenter may not possess a strong, relaxed delivery style. Without exceptional presentation skills and communication techniques, audiences quickly lose interest and may even head for the nearest exit.

Experienced presenters communicate effectively with their audiences using both verbal and nonverbal techniques. This step provides the basics of each technique to enable you to communicate your message through a variety of methods.

Verbal Communication Skills

Verbal communication can immediately engage or turn off your audience. For example, do you sound like John Wayne or Minnie Mouse? Do presentation jitters cause you to speak as fast as an auctioneer? Here are some tips to improve and hone your basic verbal communication skills.

The Four Ps—Projection, Pitch, Pronunciation, and Pace

Voice inflection can be one of your best assets in capturing the audience's attention and holding their interest. In any presentation, how you say something is just as important as what you are saying. To improve your verbal communication, consider sharpening these skills:

◆ **Projection**—your audience has to be able to hear you in every part of the room when you present. Here's a simple way to ensure that you are projecting accurately: Before your presentation have someone stand in the farthest reaches of the room, begin your presentation, and ask if he or she can hear you. Then adjust your projection as necessary. Keep in mind that it is easier for the person in the back of the room to hear during a practice session than when the room is full of people, shifting their weight on creaky chairs and rustling papers. Be prepared to ratchet up your voice projection and avoid inadvertently dropping the volume after the first few sentences of your presentation.

◆ **Pitch**—the dreaded monotone voice has lulled many a participant to sleep. When presenting, avoid droning on and be sure to modulate the pitch of your voice up or down. Having a monotone delivery is usually the result of paying more attention to saying the exact words listed on your notes rather than listening to how you are saying the words. Let the audience hear from your pitch when you are excited about something in the presentation. Modulate the pitch of your voice to accentuate more serious information. Your audience will take its cues not only from what you say, but how you say it.

◆ **Pronunciation**—if your audience can't understand what you are saying, it's as if you didn't say it at all. Successful presenters demonstrate exceptional diction—that is, the art of speaking precisely so that each word is clearly heard and understood to its fullest. Be sure to enunciate each

How Fast Do You Speak?

Before you can feel comfortable controlling your pace, you need to know the rate at which you speak. Time yourself for one minute reading the following passage aloud at your natural pace. Mark the point in the text at which you stop. Ignore the asterisks.

Disney's Epcot Center in Florida is filled with technological marvels. A tour of the international pavilions offers sights, *sounds, and smells from around the globe. The last few haunting notes from an Irish flute float across air flavored delicately *with the hint of saffron from India. Visitors talk of the amazing laser and fireworks show of the previous evening and of the *astonishing things they have seen today. There's already a waiting list for lunch at the Swiss restaurant. And over in the *Italian courtyard, a group congregates around a place in the square. The crowd grows in size and yet is strangely silent, their *attention drawn by perhaps the most amazing marvel of all—a human being stands in the square and tells a story. In the *midst of all of the most marvelous array in Epcot that technology and the famous Disney imagination can offer, we can still be *spellbound by the single storyteller, the person with a powerful message. Today's presenter is part of a rich and respected tradition.*

STEP 6

This passage is approximately 200 words long. (Words are counted based on an average unit of five spaces in text). The asterisks mark 25-word units. How many words did you read in a minute?

Normal conversation ranges from 125 to 175 words per minute. Slower than that, and listeners lose the train of thought; faster and they have a hard time hearing everything you say. Tape several minutes of your presentation, including the opening minute, several minutes at different points in the presentation, and the closing. Count the word units to determine how quickly you speak from the podium.

word clearly when presenting. In certain parts of the country, slight dialects may be difficult to understand until your ears get attuned to the sound and how specific words are pronounced. Keep this in mind if you have an accent or when presenting in certain areas in the country or abroad.

◆ **Pace**—good presenters adjust their rate of speaking to accentuate a feeling or mood. Although the average rate of speech is about 140 words per minute, to show enthusiasm or energy for a particular point, try increasing the amount of words accordingly. To make an important point perfectly clear or to emphasize something, try slowing down the rate to 100 words per minute. This isn't science, so you don't have to get out a stopwatch and count. Rather, understand that you can create a mood and atmosphere for your presentation just by how you use your voice.

Pauses and Fillers

Pauses can add more emphasis in just the right parts of any presentation. For example, a carefully placed pause can help to focus attention before you present a new key or supporting point. Pauses after you present a new idea also provide time for the audience to think about what you're saying. Pauses are also effective after you have posed a question to the audience. By pausing and remaining silent, you encourage the audience to share their thoughts or provide feedback.

Fillers—those words that creep into your presentation and fill the silence while you are thinking or transitioning to a new thought include uhs, ums, ers, ahs, okay, right, and you know. Filler words are one of the fastest ways to annoy your audience and even turn their focus to jotting down tick marks every time you use a filler word. Don't be afraid to pause and leave silence between your sentences and thoughts. Skilled, confident presenters are comfortable with the occasional silence and use it effectively to their advantage. Do not feel compelled to fill every silent moment with a filler word.

So how can you break your "filler word" habit? Write the filler word(s) to avoid on one side of a name tent or an index card. Prop the card in front of you—so that only you can see what is written on the card. Practice your speech with the card in front of you. If needed, find a friendly critic to listen to the presentation while you rehearse and "count" how often you are using these filler words.

POINTER

Use the pause for emphasis. AVOID the fillers. Be comfortable with silence.

Nonverbal Communication Skills

Body language—meaning how you look and move—can enhance or undermine your presentation. Based on different studies, it is usually accepted that between 7 and 10 percent of the effectiveness of a presentation comes from the words the presenter uses. Since the remaining 90 percent of presentation effectiveness is attributed to nonverbal communication, presenters need to be cognizant of their body language and use gestures, eye contact, and facial expressions to enhance their message. The next section provides tips and techniques to help you master and hone your nonverbal communication skills.

Body Language and Gestures

Many new presenters struggle with exactly what they should be doing with their hands and bodies when they present. For example, should they lean on or grip the lectern for security? Rock or sway? Stand poker straight with hands at their sides? Cross their arms in front of their chests? The answer is—none of these!

Effective use of body language and gestures contributes to communication—to emphasize, show agreement, and maintain audience interest. As a result it is important to consider and plan what message you want to send as you make body movements while

STEP 6

presenting, In general, use movement when you want to convey enthusiasm and energy about a particular point in your presentation. Some seasoned presenters walk to different parts of the room while making eye contact with the audience. Movement can be used to engage all the members of the audience, especially if you approach different areas of the room to make personal contact with the participants. This technique keeps everyone focused on you, including those who might be in back corners or the far recesses of the room.

Movement keeps the audience's eyes on you. Use it to engage all members of your audience.

Movement can be used to make a point or draw attention to something going on in part of the room, such as a participant asking a question. By moving in a purposeful way during the presentation, you help to maintain the audience's interest and to keep the presentation flowing.

Gestures refer to hand and body movements that are part of any presentation. When you watch a play, the actors use gestures to convey emotions, add emphasis to particular points, paint a mental picture, and so on. Important points to remember about body language and gestures include

◆ **Use quick, positive, energetic movements**—of the hands, arms, and head. Keep the attention of your audience by making your movements unpredictable. Make your gestures purposeful, for example, walk rapidly, but alter the pace of your stride as you make points and reinforce them. Coordinate movement and gestures with your delivery.

◆ **Take a natural stance**—but do not look too casual. This is very important when presenting. You want to project a comfortable, confident image, but not look too casual. As a general rule, stand with legs about 18 inches apart or so (depending on your size), equally distribute your weight on each foot, with your arms in a comfortable position at your sides or lightly resting on the lectern with your notes in view.

◆ **Pay attention to and eliminate unconscious body language**—some gestures and movements can distract the audience including fidgeting, pacing, clicking a pen cap, and jingling keys or coins in pockets.

◆ **Use gestures for emphasis**—for example, if you say, "There are three steps in creating an effective opening," hold up three fingers sequentially as you articulate each point.

◆ **Observe the audience's body language**—facial expressions, down-turned eyes, looks of concern, fidgeting, or slouching are all signs of boredom, disinterest, or lack of understanding.

◆ **Use positive facial expressions**—including smiles, expressive eyes, a look of concern, empathy, and encouragement. Look at your face in the mirror. How do you communicate feelings and emotions? How do you use your eyes, eyebrows, and mouth to express yourself?

◆ **Never sit behind a desk or stand behind a podium**—during your presentation. This establishes a barrier between you and your audience. Put more life into your presentation by moving freely about the room and down the aisles. Presenters who trap themselves behind the podium and venture out occasionally to write on a flipchart appear less than enthusiastic.

◆ **Walk toward participants as they respond**—to your questions. This encourages them to continue. As a participant responds, nod your head slowly to show you hear what they are asking. If you need to think through what he or she has asked or need to clarify the question, consider paraphrasing the question back to them or say, "So if I understand your question, you are asking . . . "

Above all, demonstrate enthusiasm and passion about the topic and the opportunity to present. Your enthusiasm is contagious and often generates interest and positive feelings from the audience.

Eye Contact and Facial Expressions

Making eye contact and exaggerating or animating your facial expressions shows the audience that you are engaging with them. Keep in mind that the larger the audience—the more you may need to exaggerate your expressions and body movements for them to be seen by the people in the back of the room.

POINTER

Do not forget to smile! A smile can pay dividends—it can be interpreted as a sign of your confidence, commitment, and interest.

So how much eye contact is appropriate? As a general rule, spend five or six seconds of eye contact at least once with each member of your audience, making sure that you look at everyone when presenting to a small group and to small pockets of people in a larger audience. Eye contact also offers an opportunity for a presenter to get a feel for how his or her audience is reacting to the presentation. By making eye contact and seeing people's expressions, the presenter can often gauge the audience's interest.

Facial expressions convey emotion and provide the presenter with the power to change the mood in the room simply by changing the look on his or her face. One of the easiest actions to take while presenting is smiling. In addition, a smile can pay dividends, too. Smiles are often interpreted by your audience as a sign of confidence, commitment, and interest in ensuring that the audience understands the presentation message. Although some presenters find it difficult to smile and talk at the same time, it is a skill worth practicing!

Using Microphones

Microphones are wonderful inventions that allow audiences to hear presentations. Although they may seem easy to use, many presenters make mistakes that cost time and cause embarrassment. There are three types of microphones that you'll likely encounter:

Body Language Don'ts

Good body language will help you to appear confident and knowledgeable. Poor body language can ruin all of the presentation writing and rehearsing in one fell swoop. When rehearsing and getting ready to take the podium, consider these body language "don'ts."

◆ Don't lean on or grip the lectern.
◆ Don't rock or sway in place.
◆ Don't stand poker straight or immobile.
◆ Don't use a single gesture repeatedly.
◆ Don't cross your arms in front of your chest.
◆ Don't use obviously practiced or stilted gestures.
◆ Don't chew gum or eat candy.
◆ Don't click or tap a pen, pencil, or pointer.
◆ Don't lean into the microphone.
◆ Don't shuffle notes unnecessarily.
◆ Don't tighten or otherwise play with your clothing.
◆ Don't crack your knuckles.
◆ Don't examine or bite your fingernails.
◆ Don't jangle change or keys.

Handheld Microphones

Most handheld microphones these days are wireless, but you can still run into some that are attached to an amplifier via a long, cumbersome cord that can make you feel anchored to your stage. Here are some tips on using handheld microphones:

◆ Don't forget that you have a microphone. Every sound, whether it's a whispered remark to a colleague, a cough, or an accidental bump against the microphone, is heard by the audience.

◆ Test the sensitivity of the microphone—before the audience arrives! No one likes to be subjected to the presenter repeating, "Test 1-2-3." Find the right distance between your mouth and the microphone to avoid feedback and ensure that your audience can hear you.

◆ Try to be natural holding the microphone and think of it as an extension of your hand.

Lavaliere Microphones

A lavaliere microphone clips to your lapel, blouse, or pocket with the transmission unit stored in your pocket or attached to your belt. A lavaliere mike allows you to walk around and speak in a natural manner. Most are wireless, but again, you may run across microphones that are still attached to a cord. Here are some pointers for using lavaliere microphones:

◆ Make sure the microphone is in a position to pick up your voice before you present.

◆ Turn your microphone's transmission unit off when you're not using it. One colleague went to use the restroom and forgot to turn off the transmission unit! Again, noise and perhaps embarrassing comments might be heard by the audience.

Podium Microphones

Some podiums have the microphone already attached—which means that you are trapped behind the podium. This fact may bother some presenters, but novice presenters often find comfort in this type of setup. When using podium microphones:

◆ Don't cling to the podium with a death grip.

◆ Don't read from your notes just because they're right there in front of you on the podium.

◆ Even if you can't move around, you can still use nonverbal communication to connect with your audience.

Now that you have reviewed the communication techniques that will enhance your presentation, use Tool 6.1 to verify that you have mastered these skills.

TOOL 6.1

Speaker's Communication-Skills Assessment

Use this checklist to self-assess an audio or videotape of your practice sessions, or have your friendly critic complete it while you rehearse or during an actual presentation. Enter the following items to indicate if you did or did not exhibit the behavior on the list.

✓   An item to indicate when you did the item on the list.

X   An item to indicate that you did not model that item.

O   An item if it did not apply to the presentation.

- ❏ Chose a title that tied audience interests to the topic
- ❏ Chose a title that established realistic audience expectations
- ❏ Used an attention-getting opening
- ❏ Presented body of the speech in an organized, logical sequence
- ❏ Used transitional words and expressions (such as then, next, despite, on the other hand) to help the audience follow the presentation sequence and flow
- ❏ Made the presentation's main theme clear
- ❏ Offered adequate substantiating arguments, statistics, examples, and so on to support the main theme
- ❏ Used words to distinguish facts and proofs ("actually," "in fact") from opinions ("I believe," "many people think")
- ❏ Used a conversational tone
- ❏ Demonstrated appropriate degree of formality
- ❏ Used personal pronouns (you, we, I)
- ❏ Explained technical terms
- ❏ Avoided jargon
- ❏ Handled notes unobtrusively
- ❏ Handled microphone professionally
- ❏ Avoided nervous gestures/postures
- ❏ Made eye contact with individuals in audience
- ❏ Avoided staring at one section or person in the audience
- ❏ Used gestures that supported (rather than detracted from) words
- ❏ Used pertinent, inoffensive humor
- ❏ Spoke loudly enough
- ❏ Varied pace of speech
- ❏ Avoided speaking too fast or slow
- ❏ Paused for audience reactions
- ❏ Avoided filler words (um, er, us, right? Okay?)
- ❏ Varied pitch of voice
- ❏ Was neither shrill, squeaky, nor monotonous
- ❏ Spoke clearly
- ❏ Pronounced words correctly
- ❏ Dressed appropriately
- ❏ Met time requirements for the presentation (within five minutes)
- ❏ Presented a memorable conclusion

STEP 6

NOTES

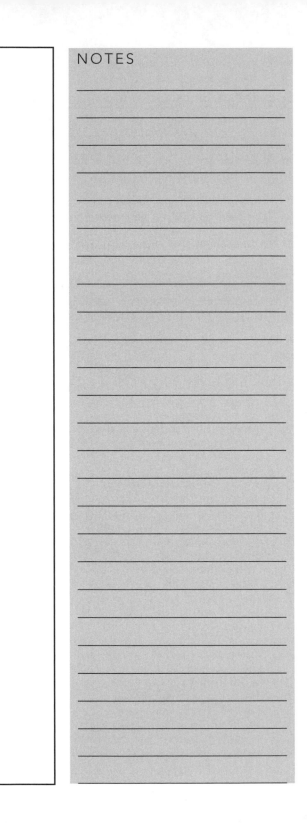

Build in Facilitation Techniques to Engage Your Audience

You've designed and developed a great presentation about a new process that not only will have a big impact on the company's bottom line but will make completing daily tasks easier for everyone who touches the process. This is a huge win for the organization and you just know that the audience will be as excited as you are as soon as they hear your message. You present the information—wait for cheers—and instead could hear crickets chirping. In your mind, you think, "Hmm, why don't they get it?" "Why aren't they asking questions?" "Why aren't they asking more about how this will change their daily tasks for the better?"

Perhaps they didn't pick up on key points of your presentation—or perhaps they didn't know that it was OK to ask questions. Sometimes presenters face big barriers preventing interactive discussions because of time constraints, setup of the facility, group size, organizational culture, and so on. Whatever the reason, successful presenters know how to use their effective communication skills to encourage participation naturally.

STEP 7

Facilitation is a technique used by a presenter to involve the audience and help them to learn from one another through open sharing of thoughts, opinions, and ideas. In the role of facilitator, the presenter uses such techniques as questioning, silence, paraphrasing, and various nonverbal cues to encourage audience participation.

Characteristics of Effective Facilitators

Some presenters are natural-born facilitators who intuitively know how to apply certain techniques to engage an audience and elicit participation. For others, a sound understanding of effective facilitation techniques and practice is all that is required. Effective facilitators are able to

◆ create an open environment by encouraging people to participate in the presentation and learning, while maintaining people's self-esteem

◆ set guidelines for audience participation, by respecting others' thoughts and ideas, ensuring that there are no unnecessary interruptions, and staying on point

◆ acknowledge people who participate by praising and thanking them for their contributions and encouraging them to continue to participate

◆ create transitions between questions asked and answered by audience members, as well as between topics

◆ be honest with what they know and don't know; acknowledging what is opinion and what is fact

◆ express an opinion when appropriate but make sure that audience members' feelings and opinions are not being judged as invalid or wrong

◆ give everyone an opportunity to participate but never forces anyone who chooses not to

STEP **7**

◆ keep the discussion flowing and on target while recognizing when to end a discussion and move on.

Encouraging Participation with Facilitation Techniques

Successful presenters leverage myriad facilitation techniques and master *when* to use a particular technique as much as *how* to use it. By understanding the basics of each technique and when to apply them, you will add more arrows in your quiver and deliver a powerful presentation that provides value to participants. Some basic facilitation techniques include

◆ **Asking questions**—this is probably the most common way to encourage participation from a group—and is a skill that serves business professionals both inside and outside of a meeting room. There are several types of questions including open-ended, closed, hypothetical, and rhetorical.

◆ **Listening**—if you expect the audience to participate, then you need to be sure to listen to what they are saying. After posing a question, pause and give them time to think and formulate their responses. When someone begins to respond, avoid *assuming* that you know what he or she is going to say. Nothing turns an audience off faster than a presenter who interrupts or jumps to hasty conclusions about a particular point—which may be incorrect. Pose a question, give the audience time to think, and then truly listen to participant input.

◆ **Accepting different opinions and views**—if you are asking for ideas, comments, and thoughts on a topic, then be prepared for views that differ from yours. If you don't agree with something, be sure that you do not leave the audience with the impression that you agree or that the information is correct if it is not. If answers to questions aren't quite on target, then redirect the question and open it up to others by asking, "What do the rest of you think?"

◆ **Silence**—silence is an effective facilitation technique and one that novice presenters often struggle with the most.

Pausing enables the audience to process what you are saying and to form their own thoughts and opinions.

This next section delves into each of these techniques to help you to hone your facilitation skills.

Questioning Techniques

Not every presentation that you make will require you to facilitate discussions. However, for today's business professionals the ability to facilitate discussions is often an expected part of business acumen. As a result, it is crucial for every business professional to know how to use various facilitation techniques. The ability to ask strong questions requires skill, practice, and planning.

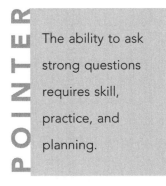

POINTER

The ability to ask strong questions requires skill, practice, and planning.

Open-Ended Questions

Open-ended questions usually require participants to respond using more than one word. These questions enable the audience to express their thoughts, ideas, feelings, and opinions.

For example, what if the presenter at the beginning of this chapter had stated at the start of the presentation that he was not only excited about the upcoming process changes, but wanted to ensure that there was plenty of time during the session for the audience to ask questions to clarify their understanding. If the presenter stated the expectation up front and then sprinkled open-ended questions throughout the presentation, the level of interactivity and enthusiasm of the audience about the process change may have been dramatically different.

For example:

◆ "With a show of hands, how many of you currently spend at least 30 minutes each day on _____ process? An hour? More than an hour?"

- "Based on what we've discussed so far, how do you think this new process will affect your job?"
- "What do you think you need to be successful with this new process change?"
- "How do you think that you can begin to implement this process change now?"

Asking an open-ended question is an excellent way of getting the audience involved in the presentation. It increases the energy level of the session and generates group synergy. Open-ended questions often start with

- "Tell me about . . . "
- "Why . . . "
- "What do you think about . . . "
- "How . . . "

Usually questions that start this way help the audience to expound on their answers, revealing information that can be helpful in discussion.

Closed-Ended Questions

Closed-ended questions are sometimes preferable to open-ended ones in certain situations. Closed-ended questions are excellent for getting at specific facts and information.

For example, what if members of the audience were expected to read information about the new process change prior to attending the presentation. You could ask a closed-ended question requiring a yes or no response to gauge how many read the information, such as: "How many of you had a chance to read the information that I sent about the new process change last week?" You aren't interested at this point whether or not they agree with or are excited about the change, only the percentage of the group that has some baseline understanding of your presentation content.

Closed-ended questions often begin with

- "Who . . . ?"
- "Where . . . "
- "When . . . "
- "Did you . . . "

Hypothetical Questions

Hypothetical questions are great to get people thinking freely in situations in which many answers may be valid. They often start with "What if . . . ?"

For example, "What if we could implement a new process regarding _____ that would reduce the amount of time you spend on that task by 50 percent every day?" or "Where do you think this process will affect your workflow the most each day?"

Hypothetical questions are excellent discussion starters because they allow the audience to internalize a situation, think through any issues, problems, or solutions, and then actively discuss the impact and their ideas. One warning—since hypothetical discussions are so effective at getting the audience to open up and join in the discussion, as a presenter you may need to reign things in a bit to meet your time constraints.

Rhetorical Questions

Rhetorical questions—although really not questions at all—are used primarily to get your audience thinking when you don't expect them to answer the question aloud. These types of questions are used primarily for effect and to create excitement or interest in the presentation content to come.

For example, "We've all heard about the new process change and I know that change is sometimes difficult. But what if I told you that this new process has been proven to reduce workflow downtime by 50 percent?"

The success of rhetorical questions, just like the other facilitation techniques discussed in this section, is directly related to *how* you ask the question as much as what you ask. When using this technique, vary the pace of your speech to emphasize key words and then end with silence. Allow the audience time to process what you have said since rhetorical questions are a great way to prime an audience to hear the key and supporting points of your presentation.

Question and Answer Sessions

Many presentations include "Q&A" sessions—meaning, a designated amount of time and a place in the presentation when the audience can ask you questions about a particular topic. For many presenters, these sessions can instill butterflies and cause knocking knees. If that sounds like you, but sure to read the sidebar called "Taking the Dread Out of Q&A."

Q&A sessions provide an excellent opportunity for a presenter to not only "show his or her stuff," but also to self-evaluate the effectiveness of the presentation based on the type of questions posed from the audience. Usually the presenter controls when the Q&A will occur, whether during the presentation or at the end. To help you decide where Q&A should be placed in the structure of the presentation, ask yourself three questions:

- ◆ **What is the purpose of my presentation?**
  If your presentation is a "need to know" and not just a "nice to know," try your best to work in at least some time for questions during the presentation.
- ◆ **How much time do I have to deliver the presentation?**
  If you are constrained by time limits and have a lot of important content to convey, then you may wish to hold Q&A until the end of the session to ensure that you have enough time to get through the requisite information. Be

sure to set this up in the beginning by saying, "After my presentation, we'll have a little time for questions."

◆ **How large is the group?**

A large, eager group plus limited time often leads to many questions. If you are going to start a Q&A session, set a time when you will stop—and stick to it.

Pointers for Conducting Q&A Sessions

Here are some pointers to remember as you conduct a Q&A session:

◆ Think before asking your question; know what your goal is and what information you seek.

◆ Ask the question first and then allow the audience enough time (at least six to eight seconds) to respond.

◆ Do a quick check for understanding. If you get confused looks, try rephrasing the question.

◆ Be careful not to single out one person to answer the question before you ask it.

◆ Wait for hands to go up, and choose someone who you think knows the answer.

◆ Don't call on the same people over and over or you'll run the risk of discouraging the rest of the group from asking questions.

◆ When calling on people to answer questions, address them by first name when possible.

◆ If someone's answer is clearly off base or seems to indicate that he or she didn't quite understand the question, very gently let the person off the hook by asking it again in a slightly different way. For example, "That's one way of looking at it, but what I was asking about was . . . "

◆ Thank the person for answering the question and move on.

Guidelines for Answering Questions from the Audience

Consider these guidelines when answering questions posed by the audience:

◆ When creating or practicing your presentation, anticipate the questions that might be asked and plan your response.

Taking the Dread Out of Q&A

Questions during presentations have two purposes: 1) to clarify information that is unclear to audience members for any reason, and 2) to engage an audience, secure their participation, and maintain communication.

Presenters often wait until the end of the session to entertain questions and announce the segment by asking, "Are there any questions?" This method is often the least useful and tends to silence serious question-askers, who might be a bit fearful of asking a question in front of a large group.

When responding to questions:
- honor each question with a direct answer and specifics
- break down complicated questions into understandable pieces
- recognize the question-askers by pointing to or describing them (for example, "Yes, the gentleman in the blue shirt . . . ")
- quickly defer irrelevant questions, but do it pleasantly
- recognize questions from all parts of the room.

- Before answering, make sure that you understand the question. If not, ask for clarification.
- Consider repeating the question for large audiences and rooms to ensure that everyone heard the question before you respond.
- If possible, plan for a wireless microphone to be available to pass around in large group sessions to facilitate a quick and smooth Q&A session and ensure that everyone can hear the questions asked.
- If you don't know an answer, add it to the parking lot and tell the audience member that you will find out the answer as soon as possible.

- Keep answers brief and to the point. If you prattle on about statistics, large amounts of data, or complicated information you will confuse and possibly lose your audience.
- After answering a question, check the audience's body language and facial expressions to see if your answer was clear. Clarify if necessary.
- Always thank the person who asked the question.

Worksheet 7.1 will help you plan the facilitation techniques that will work best with your presentation. It will also test your listening skills so you can maximize your effectiveness during Q&A sessions.

Listening to Verbal and Nonverbal Messages

Effective facilitators not only know how to appropriately structure and ask questions at precisely the right time, but they are also extremely good listeners. Active listening, while especially useful during Q&A sessions, requires concentration. You are not only employing auditory skills to listen to the words used in posing the question, but also paying attention to the underlying emotion expressed. This part of the message is often reflected in the person's tone of voice or inflection as well as nonverbal messages, such as facial expression and gesture. This underlying message usually reflects the true meaning of what is being expressed.

For example, how often have you asked a friend or co-worker if she or he understands something and while getting an affirmative "yes" or nod, you see a look of confusion or a wrinkled brow that indicates otherwise?

Good facilitators use paraphrasing—a technique of repeating back (in their own words) to an audience member what they think was asked—as an effective technique for verifying that the presenter and the audience all heard the question correctly. Paraphrasing also helps you to "buy time" as well by pausing, repeating the question, and giving you time to think through the answer.

Using Silence to Create Tension

In our society, even short periods of silence have a way of making people uncomfortable. Nevertheless, silence can be an excellent facilitation tool because it creates just enough tension to make people uncomfortable and get them thinking! The trick to using silence to your advantage is not to let people off the hook by answering for them or by rephrasing the question right away.

Keep in mind that the audience hears and processes information at a slower rate than you speak, so silence not only gives them time to let ideas and information rattle around in their heads, it is necessary when facilitating.

To use silence effectively, pose your question to the audience, then wait at least 6 to 8 seconds. If no one responds or the audience seems confused, try rephrasing the question—but do not answer for them.

For example, you could ask, "What was one challenge that you remember from the last time a new workflow change was initiated?" After your period of silence, try to rephrase the question along the lines of, "Okay, what if we narrow that down to what was one challenge that you experienced in your department as a result of the _____ workflow change?"

Advantages and Disadvantages of Questioning Techniques

Questioning provides participants with an opportunity to display their understanding of key points. Participants' responses not only tell you how effective your presentation is but also indicate how to adjust your delivery. When posing questions, you can address participants by name and involve them in presentations. Questioning also gives you the opportunity to provide positive feedback and reinforcement to ensure that participants understand the presentation content.

WORKSHEET 7.1

Facilitation Skills Worksheet

This worksheet will help you to determine which facilitation techniques you want to use during the presentation to engage participants and anticipate questions or issues. Remember, facilitation techniques are not only designed to engage the audience, but also to help facilitate learning from each other as much as from the speaker. Leverage some of the techniques in this section—including questioning, silence, paraphrasing, and nonverbal cues—to hone your skills and encourage participation.

Questioning Technique	Purpose	Include?	How can I implement this technique in the presentation?
Open-Ended Questions	Used to engage participants and have them respond with more than a yes or no answer	☐	
Closed-Ended Questions	Excellent for obtaining yes/no answers and getting at specific facts and information.	☐	
Hypothetical Questions	Used to get people thinking freely in situations where many answers may be valid. They often start with "What if . . . ?"	☐	
Rhetorical Questions	Used primarily to get your audience thinking when you don't really expect them to answer the question aloud. These types of questions are used for effect and to create excitement or interest in the presentation content to come.	☐	

Other Planning Questions:

Item	Answer
Will you have a Q&A Session?	
Are there any hot topics or pitfalls that you expect the audience to question during the presentation?	
What types of questions do you think you will field from the audience?	
What should your response be for each of the anticipated questions?	
If you cannot answer all of the audience questions, how will you help the audience to find the answer (e.g., table & follow-up via e-mail with the answers, point them to Internet or other resources for additional information)?	

Listening Self-Assessment Checklist

If you are going to take questions from the audience, you need to ensure that your listening skills are on par with those of other successful presenters. Use this self-assessment to think about your current listening skills and if you need to do anything different during the presentation.

Question	Answer
When people speak to me, I often feel that they are wasting my time.	
I tend to anticipate what someone is asking me, interrupting others, and jump in with an answer before the full question is asked.	
I have trouble listening when there is noise or a distracting activity nearby.	
When someone asks me a question, I often focus more on the next part of my presentation or the conversation rather than actively listening to the question being asked.	
I take notes to record the facts or details when someone asks a question to ensure that I have heard what is asked correctly.	
I often paraphrase a question back to the audience to ensure that I heard the question correctly and to ensure that everyone else heard the question.	
I keep my emotions under control when sensitive topics or opposing views are raised by others.	

Advantages

The use of questioning and reinforcement is useful for the following reasons:

- ◆ it involves all participants in the presentation
- ◆ it stimulates and motivates participants
- ◆ it provides participants with an opportunity to display their understanding of the topic
- ◆ it promotes active, not passive participation
- ◆ participants have an opportunity to apply the knowledge and skills you have presented
- ◆ responses to questions provide feedback as to the effectiveness of the delivery of the presentation
- ◆ the questioning process helps you to evaluate individual comprehension
- ◆ questions create variety in presentations.

Disadvantages

There are, however, some aspects of questioning and reinforcement that can detract from your presentation:

- ◆ the overuse of low-level or short-answer questions may not challenge the participants
- ◆ questioning can be time-consuming
- ◆ some participants may not wish to get involved in the interaction process
- ◆ some participants may attempt to dominate the interaction process.

Questioning and Reinforcement Techniques

Carefully formulate questions during the planning process and use the following guidelines:

1. Write questions at a variety of levels, from the simple *yes/ no* kind to those that require more thought. Questions such as "Why?" and "What is your opinion?" stimulate a lot of discussion.

2. Phrase questions carefully. Avoid ambiguous or vague questions since they may confuse participants.

3. Make questions short enough to remember.

4. Design questions to focus on key points from the presentation. Do not waste time asking about secondary or less important information. You want to be sure participants understand the most significant material.

5. Design questions so they do not suggest the answer and state them in a way that eliminates guessing.

6. State questions clearly for the entire group. Pause for a volunteer response or direct your questions to specific participants. Address participants by name, and then ask your own questions.

7. Repeat participant questions and responses, especially if you are addressing a large group. This ensures that everyone can hear. It also gives you an opportunity to clarify questions and responses and provides positive reinforcement to the participant.

8. On occasion, handle participant questions by pausing and then redirecting the question to another participant. This involves others in the discussion and creates more interaction.

STEP 7

NOTES

_____

_____

_____

_____

_____

_____

_____

_____

_____

_____

_____

_____

_____

_____

_____

_____

_____

_____

_____

_____

_____

_____

_____

_____

Practice, Practice, Practice

Rehearsing a speech

Speaking from notes vs. memorizing your speech

Tools and techniques for practicing your speech

After all the analysis and preparation is completed and the important decisions about the subject and structure of the presentation are made, the final step before giving a presentation is to practice. Practice provides an opportunity to polish all content, to rethink structure, and to rehearse materials and presentation dynamics. Practicing helps you to build confidence, and to remember the flow and key points to emphasize during the presentation. The time spent practicing is usually proportional to the level of calm you experience the day of the presentation. Knowing the material, transitions, and key points is a direct result of the time you spend practicing and preparing.

A key to practicing is to rehearse what you are going to say at the opening of the presentation. Memorize the first few paragraphs. Usually having the introduction memorized or thoroughly practiced will reduce your stress level and get your presentation started on the right foot.

Don't memorize the entire written speech unless you're sure that your memory will not fail. Many speakers' stage fright stems

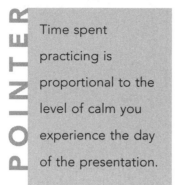

Time spent practicing is proportional to the level of calm you experience the day of the presentation.

from the fear of forgetting the *exact words* in the presentation. In most speeches, some of the words must be exact—such as direct quotations. Aside from a few words that must be exact, focus on the ideas that you want to convey. Your notes should support these key ideas. By drafting and rehearsing the presentation, you will be familiar with the content without needing to memorize it—which will also bring an air of spontaneity that makes a speech lively.

Some presenters overprepare for their presentations—they write out every word on note cards. But, if you overscript your presentation, a single question might throw you off. Other presenters take the opposite approach to their presentations and think that they can "wing it" without notes because they "know" the subject. If you use no notes, though, a momentary lapse in concentration could throw the presentation into chaos because you have nothing to help you get back on track.

The time required for you to adequately practice and prepare will vary depending on the type of presentation, your comfort level with the subject, who the audience is, and what presentation method you are most comfortable with. If you are an experienced speaker, then go with the practicing techniques that work best for you and integrate the tips in this section to help you prepare.

Throughout the speech, aim to be
◆ Honest
◆ Accurate
◆ Clear
◆ Informative
◆ Interesting.

Notice that "entertaining" is not on the list. Only a few public speakers choose to sign on for speeches that have entertainment as a main point. Seriously, you can earn fame and fortune if you have the knack of consistently entertaining audiences. Fortunately, the most that's usually required is for you to be interesting.

An audience's interest is captured by:
- Variety in a speech's content and delivery
- Movement of the speaker's face, arms, hands, or whole body
- Familiarity or novelty
- Conflict, comparisons, and contrasts
- Suspense
- Concreteness of words and examples
- Humor
- Personal involvement.

In addition to using examples that are relevant to audience needs and interests, you can involve audience members by:
- Asking rhetorical, nonaccusatory questions
- Calling for a show of hands
- Asking them to repeat a word or phrase (warning: it's embarrassing if they don't—an audience needs to warm up to you before they'll speak out, so save this technique for the middle or end of a speech)
- Directing the audience to look at something in the meeting room
- Appealing to their senses with phrases such as "Imagine a bright red . . . " "Remember hearing the whistle of . . . " or "Suppose you felt the freezing force of . . . "

Rehearsing a Speech

The first 90 seconds of a presentation are the most important because that's when the tone is set for the rest of the talk. If you start off on the right foot, chances are you'll continue along that path. If, however, you start off on the wrong foot, it can be very difficult to recover. That's why great presenters have the first 90 seconds of their presentation down pat. Once again, it's all about being prepared. When you start strong, your audience becomes energized and its interest is piqued.

Some experienced presenters start with an interesting or humorous story, slowly building to the essence of their presentation. Others hit hard with a benefit statement that makes it clear why the audience should listen to the presentation. Find your own way of starting, practice it until you know it, and then offer it. As you gain experience, you'll become more confident about adding to your repertoire of strong openings.

Once you know what you're going to say, consider some of these suggestions for that first 90 seconds:
- ◆ Look like you're confident even if your knees are shaking.
- ◆ Acknowledge your audience, smile (if appropriate), and start talking.
- ◆ Exhibit an outward appearance that says to your audience that there isn't any other place you'd rather be.
- ◆ Begin by painting a mental picture with your words and actions for the audience right from the start.
- ◆ Be focused, positive, enthusiastic, and speak confidently.

Remember, the qualities that good speakers demonstrate during presentations include
- ◆ Respect for self and for listeners
- ◆ Honesty
- ◆ Objectivity
- ◆ Sense of humor
- ◆ Adequate preparation
- ◆ A balance between confidence and modesty
- ◆ Verbal, vocal, and physical communication skills
- ◆ Appropriate appearance.

When practicing and rehearsing the speech, focus on how and where each of these qualities will most likely occur during the presentation.

Rehearse the speech three to five times and ensure that the speech has a logical flow of ideas to help bring the listeners along as you reveal each point in the presentation.

Presentations should have the following components. Verify that the flow of the presentation supports the outlined structure and that the key points are clearly conveyed as the presentation unfolds from the introduction, the body, and the close. Transitions should help listeners follow your flow and rationale.

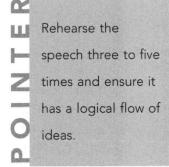

POINTER

Rehearse the speech three to five times and ensure it has a logical flow of ideas.

◆ **Introduction**—this should be consistent with what has been publicized about you and the title, and explains why you are qualified to speak on the subject, what your view of the subject is, and why you believe this audience should hear about it.

◆ **Body-supporting material**—within subtopics, plan a priority order for presenting information so that you have flexibility in how long you speak. Sometimes, an earlier agenda runs longer than expected and your time may be cut back. Other times, for example, when another scheduled speaker cancels, you may be asked to speak for a longer time. Finally, the audience reaction to your speech—sleepy nods and attentive stares and chuckles—may also dictate whether you stop the presentation sooner than planned or give the presentation in its entirety.

◆ **A short conclusion**—the surest way to get applause is to stop talking. In fact, if you get applause during the presentation, then rest assured that your speech is a success.

If the presentation includes audiovisuals, then be sure to incorporate them when you practice so that you become comfortable with them. Practice smooth transitions in

◆ referring to specific page numbers in handouts
◆ knowing when to display the next slide

STEP 8

◆ knowing how many times you need to advance a slide for all of the animation or special elements to appear (for example, a red circle appearing over a specific section of a form or numbers on a spreadsheet to orient listeners to what you are referring to).

If you'll be speaking from behind a lectern, try rehearsing behind a turned-around chair or a music stand. If you're not 5'6" or taller, try to find out exactly how tall the lectern will be. You may need to bring a platform to stand on so you and the audience can see one another and so that you can reach the mike. If you'll be using a hand mike, practice using a real one or holding a wire whisk or spoon a few inches from your mouth. If the real microphone you'll use has a long cord, consider tying a rope to your makeshift mike. Practice pulling the cord behind you, and backtracking without tripping over it.

Speaking from Notes versus Memorizing Your Speech

Do you have nightmares about approaching a podium before an audience and forgetting what to say, dropping or frantically shuffling through your notes, or spilling water on your notes so they are an illegible blot?

Well, worry no more. Put all reminders on two to six numbered notecards. Carry two sets. If you drop a card(s), switch to set two (which you keep in a pocket; don't put both sets on the lectern). Use 3" × 5" or 4" × 6" file cards printed with large, dark letters. Use all capitals to indicate major sections of the body of the speech, and sentence case for subtopics within sections. If you're worried about forgetting your opening and conclusion, put key words from the opening above the first section head and write your conclusion after the last subtopic.

When you speak, put your notecards near the top of the lectern so you won't have far to look down—lessening the time you lose eye contact with your audience. If all your reminders fit on the upper two-thirds of one to three sheets of paper, you may prefer to use paper for your notes. Use slightly stiff, high-quality paper that won't rattle into the mike.

What should go on your note cards or pages? Weed through the key points of your speech—if you wrote it out in its entirety. Think about the organization of the topics and subtopics and rearrange slightly if needed, for clarity. If, after rehearsing several times, you still struggle with the appropriate setup or transition to move from one topic to the next, write a "T" or "transition" on the card with a few key words to help you remember the key point our setup to the next sequence of presentation content.

After adequate practice and rehearsing, you'll probably be able to condense the number of file cards further. If needed, put little symbols (for example, smiley face) or notes to remind you to smile and make eye contact. If you tend to "zip" through a particular section of the speech and want to remind yourself to slow your pace in a particular section, perhaps draw a snail or a clock to encourage yourself to slow down and give the audience time to digest your message and think.

POINTER

Put symbols or notes on your cards to remind you to smile and make eye contact with the audience.

STEP **8**

Tools and Techniques for Practicing Your Speech

Nothing helps you to overcome nervousness better than knowing your material. To accomplish this goal, consider using some of these techniques to practice before a presentation. Tool 8.1 will help you determine what your strengths and weaknesses are as you practice.

TOOL 8.1
Presenter and Presentation Qualities Assessment

Use this checklist to self-assess an audio or videotape of your practice sessions, or have your friendly critic complete it while you rehearse your presentation. By separating the presenter from the presentation, you can hone both before the curtain goes up!

Presenter Qualities

Insincere, Jumpy	1 2 3 4 5 6 7 8 9 10	Believable
Limp, Passive	1 2 3 4 5 6 7 8 9 10	Dynamic
Uneasy, Awkward	1 2 3 4 5 6 7 8 9 10	Comfortable
Uninterested, Detached	1 2 3 4 5 6 7 8 9 10	Enthusiastic
Uninterested, Shallow	1 2 3 4 5 6 7 8 9 10	Knowledgeable
Overly Formal or Serious	1 2 3 4 5 6 7 8 9 10	Appropriate Humor
Reads Text/Avoids Eye Contact	1 2 3 4 5 6 7 8 9 10	Good Eye Contact
Monotone, Lacks Vocal Color	1 2 3 4 5 6 7 8 9 10	Skilled Voice Variety

Presentation Qualities

Rambling, Unclear Focus	1 2 3 4 5 6 7 8 9 10	Clear Focus or Purpose
Canned / Overly General	1 2 3 4 5 6 7 8 9 10	Tailored to Group / Occasion
Haphazard / Jumpy	1 2 3 4 5 6 7 8 9 10	Clearly, Logically Developed
Too Long or Short	1 2 3 4 5 6 7 8 9 10	Appropriate Length
Data Dump / Overwhelming	1 2 3 4 5 6 7 8 9 10	Memorable
Too Formal / Academic / Complex	1 2 3 4 5 6 7 8 9 10	Understandable
Pushy / Hard Sell / Railroading	1 2 3 4 5 6 7 8 9 10	Realistic in Scope
Pointless, Lackluster	1 2 3 4 5 6 7 8 9 10	Challenging

STEP **8**

◆ **Practice in front of a mirror**—some people find this technique helpful, but it may subtly reinforce the notion that you're talking to and for yourself rather than the audience.

◆ **Use a tape recorder**—this tool can be a good way to check your voice and diction. You can also listen to the tape while driving or doing other things to assess if your voice, pace, pauses, clarity, and flow are on target with what you want to deliver. If you are seriously self-conscious about your taped voice, don't use a recorder since you might overreact to minor problems and undermine your confidence.

◆ **Use a video camera**—this tool gives you an opportunity to observe your body language as well as hear yourself; however, like a tape recorder, a video camera may discourage some people when reviewing the video.

◆ **Employ a friendly critic**—this technique puts the emphasis on projecting to an audience. Be sure that the critic understands what you are trying to do and his or her role in providing you with feedback or reacting to the presentation. For example, if you have determined that your audience prefers a casual tone, you shouldn't be criticized for lack of formality.

◆ **Practice the speech aloud**—practice pronouncing difficult words (or eliminate them), test your pace and time the speech to see if your delivery is within the time allotted for your subject. Don't worry too much about over-rehearsing, you'll know when it's time to stop.

◆ **Focus on nonverbal aspects**—although most people practice their presentations focusing on the verbal delivery, remember to practice the nonverbal aspects as well. Practice making eye contact (looking away from your notes and at different points around the room), using hand gestures, voice inflection, and your body language in general.

◆ **Hire a professional speech consultant/trainer**—the help of a professional is worthwhile if you have:

STEP **8**

◆ an extreme case of stage fright (terror as opposed to normal nerves)

◆ a strong accent not understood by audiences outside your language community even after they've been listening for two or three minutes

◆ a concern that lack of speaking skill is limiting your career potential.

◆ **Have a dress rehearsal**—find out if you can schedule time to practice or have a dress rehearsal in the room where the presentation will be given. Even if you cannot rehearse in the presentation location, be sure to practice with visuals, handouts, and all materials that you will use to synchronize them with the presentation. This is especially true if you add any audiovisuals to the presentation.

◆ **Find a friendly audience**—this route to improvement takes time but informs you of the range of audience responses your speech inspires. Consider enrolling in your local branch of Toastmasters International, learning their advice for "speechcrafters," and honing your skills in the company of other developing speakers.

STEP

8

STEP

8

Pause and Refresh—Relax, You'll Do Fine

Does the thought of having to give a presentation immediately bring up thoughts of stage fright, presentation jitters, nervousness, butterflies, fretting, anxiety, and foreboding? If so, keep in mind that it is natural to be nervous before giving a presentation. Almost everyone gets butterflies—the trick is to harness this nervous energy and direct it into delivering a stellar presentation.

Whatever you do, do not start off by saying, "Whew, am I nervous!" and broadcasting your fear. Participants will then look for nervous signals during your presentation rather than listening to your message. The tips and tricks offered in this chapter can help you to steady your nerves and get in the right frame of mind prior to stepping on the podium.

Using Techniques to Steady Your Nerves and Make Your Presentation a Success

An expectant hush falls on the crowd. Offstage, the speaker breathes deeply. The introducer's voice rings clearly through the giant room, giving brief highlights of the speaker's credentials. The speaker strides confidently to the stage, pauses, looks out across the audience, and begins.

The presentation is an ideal blend of intriguing topic and informative content, which inspires a sense of immediacy in the listeners. A preview of the key points helps the audience listen most effectively. Each key point is supported by distilled information and vivid examples. The content brims with value, relevance, and timeliness; the delivery is animated, yet relaxed. The presenter uses a compelling voice, direct eye contact, and occasional humor to engage and hold the audience. Visuals, handouts, and reference material reinforce the message. Audience questions are handled with skill, intelligence, and respect. The presentation finishes with a challenge and a call to action.

One technique—as illustrated in the example above—called "visualization," is used by many successful presenters to rehearse in their heads not only the flow of the presentation but also how the presenter delivers the content as well as the audience's reaction at each point in the speech.

Remember, it's normal to be nervous. In fact, if you aren't at least a little nervous, you need to seriously question whether you are ready to give a presentation, because nerves give you the "edge" that often gets the adrenaline going and can make the difference between a good presentation and an outstanding, engaging presentation!

Use these additional techniques to help steady your nerves before the presentation:

◆ **Plan what you are going to wear**—plan to wear something that you always feel comfortable in, that should be a little more formal than the most formally dressed person you expect in the audience. Do not choose to wear anything new the day of the presentation, including suits, haircuts, shoes, jewelry, and so on. If you are uncomfortable, it will add to your nervousness and distract you from the task at hand.

◆ **Try to arrive at least 15–30 minutes early**—to familiarize yourself with your surroundings and the layout of the room, to ensure that the room is set up as planned, and to deal with any potential issues (for example, are the audiovisual aids available and working).

◆ **Use a preparation checklist**—have a "cheat sheet checklist" ready to go so that you have a standard routine that includes checking all audiovisual equipment, room setup, other logistics, additional information from the sponsor (e.g., we need to shave 10 minutes off your presentation or we need you to speak 20 minutes longer than planned), revised numbers of participants, handling of late arrivals, getting a glass or bottle of water, and anything else that will alleviate possible pot holes.

◆ **Use a crutch to help you with the flow or key points**—for some presenters, crutches might be audiovisual aids, flipcharts, or notes formatted with specific colors, highlighted text, and so on. Whatever works for you, don't be afraid to use crutches to help keep you grounded on the flow of the topics and key points. If you get distracted or lose your place in the presentation your crutch will help to get you back on track.

◆ **Do some deep breathing**—use deep-breathing techniques by inhaling through your nose, holding your breath for a few seconds, and slowly exhaling through your mouth. This technique gets more oxygen circulating throughout your body and your brain.

◆ **Do some warm-up exercises**—along with deep breathing while out of sight of the audience (for example, waiting to

STEP 9

be introduced), do some head or shoulder rolls, arm- and side-stretches, or even a few toe touches to stretch, warm up your body, and relax. For example, pull your shoulders up toward your ears and then push them down. Shake out cold hands to stimulate them and warm them up. If you can't do any of these because you are in front of the audience, take one last deep breath before speaking into the mike.

- **Envision the first 90 seconds**—use your visualization technique to play the first 90 seconds of your presentation in your head again to get your focused.

- **Greet audience members as they arrive**—depending on the size of the audience, this may or may not be feasible. If you can meet and greet the participants as they enter, this may help to reduce your stress level and provide you with insight into their motivation for attending.

- **You lose your place or an audience member asks a "stumper" question**—it is OK to take a few seconds to find your place, gather your thoughts or ponder a question that someone has asked. Consider calmly taking a sip of water, glancing at your notes, or formulating your answer to a sticky question. Sometimes "pregnant pauses" not only allow you to gather your thoughts but also allow the audience members to noodle over the question asked or the information presented. Keep in mind that presenters usually speak faster than audience members can process the information, so slight pauses not only help you, but also allow the audience time to think a well.

Harnessing the Power of Positive Thinking

Positive thinking helps with stress management and can even improve your presentation delivery. Positive thinking focuses on being optimistic in your approach and attitude.

So how can you put this into action to develop successful presentation skills? Positive thinking focuses on "self-talk," which is the stream of thoughts running through your mind every day. These thoughts can be positive or negative. So when you are going to present—don't waste energy imagining everything that could go wrong. Rather, focus on how this presentation is going to "wow" the audience!

For example, if you are worried about giving your presentation and are visualizing that you will trip across the stage, your notes will fall and be out of order, you will lose your place in the presentation, or crumble when an audience member asks a challenging question—what do you think is most likely going to happen when you take the stage?

> **POINTER**
> Positive thinking focuses on being positive in your approach and attitude. Don't waste energy imagining everything that could go wrong.

It's important to differentiate between negative and positive self-talk. Compare "I'll never be able to get up before that group and explain to them the new benefits package" with "I know what I'm talking about, and I can give this presentation so that the others will understand this new benefits package too." Using positive self-talk (and being prepared, of course) increases your chances of accomplishing your goal by quantum leaps.

Positive thinking requires behavior change and creating new habits—so just like any change, this takes time and practice. Periodically during the day, stop and reflect on what you are thinking about. Are your thoughts positive or negative? If you find that they are mostly negative, then stop and find a way to put a positive spin on them.

Focus on the visualization technique mentioned earlier in this chapter. In your mind's eye, do a "run through" of the presentation. Visualize how you want it to flow, what you plan to say, when you plan to use the visual aids, and so on. By focusing on

STEP 9

the best delivery scenario, you will be on your way to implementing positive thinking and visualizing success!

Preparing on the Day of the Presentation

On presentation day, plan to wear something:
- comfortable
- compatible with the color(s) of whatever will be behind you
- solid in color or with a small, overall pattern
- bright (for example, such as a bright-red tie or scarf near your face)
- similar to the most formal outfit you would expect audience members to wear.

Avoid
- excessive food or caffeinated beverages
- alcohol
- over-the-counter medications that may make you drowsy or hyperactive.

Remember to bring
- your note cards or pages in duplicate
- several handkerchiefs
- a small tape recorder and tape (if the sponsor hasn't arranged for professional audio- or videotaping)
- an emergency telephone number to call if you're delayed or need directions after you're on the way to the presentation location.

Keep in mind the following:
- You are always speaking to individuals no matter how many people are in the audience.
- To some degree, audience members have different backgrounds, and some of them may have different private problems you can't see (such as a toothache). Nobody (to

paraphrase Lincoln) "can please all of the people, all of the time," so if a few people in the audience look grumpy or pained, it probably has nothing to do with the quality of your presentation.

◆ Chances are, people who've made the effort to come to the presentation want to hear what you have to say and want you to succeed.

◆ You've done your homework—so you know what you're talking about.

◆ Nervous energy is a natural high that energizes speakers who don't worry about it. If your excitement threatens to turn to jitters, use up excess energy with a few small exercises or breathing techniques.

POINTER

Ten+ Deadly Mistakes

Research conducted by Meeting Planners International indicates that there are 12 presenting "sins" that prompt attendees to walk out, criticize programs harshly, send letters of complaint, or ask for their money back. They are

◆ Appearing unprepared
◆ Handling questions inappropriately
◆ Apologizing for self or organization
◆ Being unaware of current public information in his or her field
◆ Using unprofessional audiovisual aids
◆ Seeming to be off-schedule—especially failing to end on time
◆ Not involving attendees
◆ Not establishing personal rapport
◆ Appearing disorganized
◆ Not starting off quickly with impact
◆ Selling from the professional platform
◆ Using sexist or racist comments, ethnic slurs, or inappropriate humor.

STEP 9

Handling Emergencies While Presenting

Here are some quick tips and tricks of what to do if

- **You perspire profusely**—wipe your face with a handkerchief. Do it firmly, do not dab. Avoid using a tissue since it may shred and stick to your face.
- **Your hands shake**—rest them on the lectern but don't put a death grip on it!
- **Your knees wobble**—do nothing. If you're behind a lectern, no one can see. If you're at the head of a runway, walk around a bit; the shaking will stop.
- **You need to cough, sneeze, or clear your throat**—turn away from the mike; go ahead and cough. If necessary, take a sip of water before you begin again. Say "As I was saying . . . "
- **Your nose starts to run**—Say "Excuse me," turn from the mike, and blow your nose. Don't be dainty or you'll just have to do it again soon. Turn back to the mike and continue your speech. Bring two or three handkerchiefs with you, just in case.
- **You notice the audience's chairs aren't facing the lectern**—if the chairs aren't bolted down, start by saying, "I think you'll be more comfortable if your chairs are facing the speaker's stand. So, before I get started, why don't you turn them around?" Wait until the hubbub dies down, then start as you planned.
- **The audience knowledge varies and they know more than you**—knowing how much knowledge or expertise your audience has regarding the subject of your presentation will affect the breadth and depth of your presentation. At times, you might not have a good feel for this until you are meeting and greeting some of the audience members. You will need to determine if the audience needs to hear everything you are prepared to present or if you should employ the KISS principle ("keep it simple, stupid!). If the audience expertise varies widely, try to approach the topic from a middle-ground perspective so that

you provide new information to novices and sprinkle in more advanced information to provide something new to those who already have baseline knowledge of the topic. You can always adjust the pace and depth of the presentation downward, to ensure you are reaching as many people as possible. If several audience members possess PhDs and they have garnered accolades from peers or the industry on the topic, don't panic. When appropriate, solicit opinions and try to draw some of these "experts" into the discussion. Don't give control over to them—but by recognizing their expertise and opinions, you can build potential allies on the subject.

◆ **You are presenting to organizational superiors**—if the audience includes your superiors or C-level executives, involve these participants by asking them to share personal experiences about the topic, for example, which leadership traits they find most useful in their roles as managers. By establishing and encouraging this dynamic, you assume a facilitator role that builds credibility, shows off your skills, and takes the pressure off you for being the sole source of content and ideas.

Managing Q&A Sessions

Questions asked during the presentation have two purposes:

◆ to clarify matters that are for any reason unclear to the audience

◆ to engage an audience, secure their presentation, and maintain communication.

No matter what the purpose is for the question-and-answer session, you will need to stay in command of the session the entire time. Use these best practices to maintain control and effectively manage the Q&A session.

◆ Anticipate questions the audience is likely to ask. Plan short, to-the-point answers.

STEP **9**

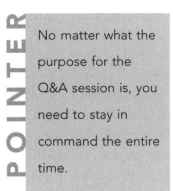

POINTER

No matter what the purpose for the Q&A session is, you need to stay in command the entire time.

◆ Announce that you'll be taking questions for 20 minutes (or whatever time is allotted), then say you'll wait a few minutes for those who need to leave now to pack up and go.

◆ Invite questions by saying something like, "Let's get started. Now, what questions do you have? To give as many people as possible a chance to speak, please limit your question to one minute."

◆ Arrange for someone you know to ask the lead-off question. Hearing someone else from the audience speak first gives other audience members time to think and psychological permission to take the floor. Admit that you know the questioner. Say, "I see my friend Sue's hand out there. Yes, Sue?"

◆ Call on people in different areas of the audience. If audience members might be categorized by gender, age, or ethic group, don't exclude that group. Also give each person you call on "equal time" up to the established limit.

◆ Listen with a neutral expression. Make eye contact with the question-asker, but avoid smiling, frowning, or nodding "yes" or "no." If you say, "That's a good question" to some people, those who do not win this praise may be disappointed. If you praise every question, you'll sound insincere.

◆ Stop long-winded question-askers. Break eye contact. Hold up your hand to indicate "stop." Say, "Let me respond to that." Say it twice if necessary. If a questioner still continues, handle this person like a heckler.

◆ Repeat questions through your mike unless:
  ◆ Question-askers have mikes of their own.
  ◆ Part of the question is something you don't want to be quoted as saying. If you repeat, "Why does XYZ Corp. fire older workers instead of retraining them?" expect

STEP 9

to hear on the news that you said "XYZ Corp. fires older workers instead of retraining them."

- Be prepared to say, "I can't answer that question because it assumes (whatever) while I believe (whatever to the contrary). This will save you from the issue mentioned above. Instead, say, "I can't answer that because you assume workers' ages were a factor. Actually, the recent layoffs were based on. . . . And workers were selected for retraining based on . . . "
- Divide multipart questions. Answer the parts separately.
- Don't challenge question-askers with "Why do you ask?" If a question seems vague or rambling, say "Could you restate that?" If after the restatement you still don't get the point, use a phrase from the restatement to construct a question that you are prepared to answer.
- Relate answers to the main point of the speech when possible.
- Control the last words the audience hears. Say, "We just have time for one or two more questions." If your next answer goes particularly well, end the session. If the question and answer are off the main point of the presentation, finish by restating the key point of the presentation.

Generating questions usually falls in a question-and-answer session at the end of the presentation. The traditional Q&A starts with the presenter asking, "Are there any questions?" However, this method may intimidate and inhibit audience members who have very serious questions from asking them in a large-group setting.

To facilitate listeners to ask questions, presenters often ask the audience to "anonymously" write questions on 3-by-5-inch cards that are passed to the speaker.

In other presentation formats, question-askers may line up at a microphone positioned at the head of the aisle before your presentation. This microphone is usually **not** activated until after your presentation. If that is the case, keep in mind that you may need to switch the "audience" microphone on from the lectern or turn it off if a participant becomes verbally abusive or refuses others to access the mike.

In other situations, someone with a hand mike may hold it out to audience members you have recognized for questions, or you may have the only microphone in the room.

When responding to participant questions:

◆ Honor each question with a direct answer. Support answers with specifics.

◆ Divide any complicated questions into understandable parts and deal with each part.

◆ When listeners ask a question in front of the group, recognize them and reiterate the question to confirm that you understand what they are asking and to ensure that everyone in the audience heard the question being asked.

◆ Quickly defer irrelevant questions, but do it pleasantly.

◆ Recognize questioners from all parts of the room, not just those who might be in the front.

Knowing that you are prepared and have considered everything you need for your presentation will enable you to focus and be calm. Use Tool 9.1 to verify that you have taken care of everything so you can be at ease.

TOOL 9.1
Countdown-to-Successful-Presentations Checklist

Use this final countdown checklist to help you relax and ensure that everything will go off without a hitch on presentation day!

2+ Weeks Before the Presentation (Start as soon as possible!)

☐ Tackle the list of 5W questions to determine the purpose of the presentation and conduct an informal audience analysis.

☐ Make the room arrangements including equipment, supplies, refreshments, etc.

☐ Create your presentation and visual aids.

☐ Select the type of facilitation techniques you want to use to create session interactivity.

☐ Develop the specific questions to ask the audience and anticipate audience questions and your planned response.

☐ Make a list of all supporting presentation materials that you need.

☐ Put together and confirm that you have everything needed in your presenter's resource / risk management kit (see Table 10.1).

☐ Do a run through and fine-tune your presentation and notes.

One Week Before the Presentation

☐ Confirm that you have the right date and time of the presentation.

☐ Confirm that the room and set-up arrangements will be ready for presentation day.

☐ Rehearse your presentation with a friendly critic and ask for feedback and ideas.

☐ Make any final adjustments to your notes and confirm that you have a backup set of notes ready to go.

☐ Memorize the first 90 seconds of your presentation and how you plan to introduce each key point during the presentation.

☐ Practice using all audiovisuals including practicing with your flipcharts, switching to overhead transparencies, or presentation software slides. Be sure to click through all of the slides to remember where any special effects—such as dissolves, animation, or sounds—occur in relation to your notes. Check for any misspellings.

☐ Pick out the clothes you plan to wear—remember, wear what you are going to be most comfortable in (preferably nothing new) that is slightly more formal than your audience.

☐ Send presentation materials and any supplies ahead of time and call to be sure that they arrived.

☐ Confirm the directions for the meeting location.

☐ Exchange phone numbers with the sponsor or contact person for the event—especially if you are flying in.

continued on next page

STEP 9

Tool 9.1, continued

❒ Double-check your presenter's toolkit (see Table 10.1, p. 171) and replenish the supplies as needed.

❒ Use your visualization techniques and positive self-talk to run through your presentation in your mind's eye and visualize success.

Presentation Day

❒ Arrive at least 30 minutes to 1 hour prior to your presentation time.

❒ Verify the presentation room location.

❒ Identify the on-site audiovisual contact or how to contact the presentation sponsor.

❒ Ask to have the box of materials that you sent ahead delivered if it is not already in the presentation room.

❒ Test all equipment.

❒ Tape down cords or power strips to prevent tripping hazards.

❒ Focus all equipment.

❒ Test the microphones, if necessary.

❒ Set the volume controls for microphones and any audiovisual aids.

❒ Have the extra set of note cards ready in your pocket and a set in place on the lectern.

❒ Organize your space for handouts and your presentation supplies such as markers, tape, and so on.

❒ Get a glass or bottle of water and paper towels.

❒ Scout out the restroom location.

❒ Arrange participant handouts either at their seats or at the end of the aisles for quick distribution either at the beginning or end of the presentation.

❒ Tidy up the room by hiding empty boxes, etc.

Before you Present

❒ Review the first 90 seconds of your opening.

❒ Do your deep breathing and stretching techniques to help you relax.

❒ Run through your visualization and envision success and how you want the session to flow.

❒ Greet the participants.

❒ Present a memorable conclusion.

STEP
9

STEP
9

Deliver a Flawless Presentation—No Matter What Happens

OVERVIEW

Counting down to a successful presentation

Resolving logistical issues

Resolving audience issues

Every presenter will face at least one day when all seems right with the world—and then the most terrible of disasters descends upon the presentation. So what will differentiate and escalate you to the status of experienced, successful speaker? Being prepared for the times when things go wrong. Nobody can anticipate everything that can go wrong, but having a contingency plan is the first step to managing and mitigating this risk.

So what should you consider when developing your contingency plan and risk-management toolkit? The following list offers a dozen steps that help you think about the plan you will implement in case things do not go as expected. Taking the time to develop this contingency plan can make the difference between calmly and systematically addressing the issue in front of an audience and utter embarrassment.

Counting Down to a Successful Presentation

1. As soon as you know you will be making a presentation, contact the individuals who will have an effect on the success of your presentation. These may include the sponsor, audiovisual coordinator, hotel or conference representative, caterer, housekeeper, and any others you can think of. Discuss what you will need and find out if any limitations will be imposed on your presentation.

2. Review all presentation materials, including the visuals and handouts, to make sure that everything is in order and ready to use.

3. Keep your presenter's contingency toolkit (see Table 10.1) equipped and ready to go at a moment's notice in case of a problem or if an item is not available at the presentation site.

4. Prior to your presentation, check with the program coordinator, the audiovisual expert, or others who helped you get ready for your presentation to ensure that they have fulfilled their supporting roles. Making friends could be a key factor in your success if something goes wrong.

5. If you are presenting off site, ship your presentation materials so that they can arrive at least two days before your presentation to make sure you have some leeway if the shipment is delayed. Use the shipper's tracking service to make sure your materials arrive on time. Don't assume anything!

6. Arrive at the presentation site at least 15 minutes prior to your presentation even if you are familiar with the location. Give yourself at least 30 minutes if your presentation is off site or at an unfamiliar location to ensure that the room is set up properly and all equipment and materials are ready to go.

TABLE 10.1

Presenter's Contingency Toolkit

❐ Duplicate set of note cards, rubber-banded and in order	❐ Index cards (especially the kind you prepared your notes on)
❐ Business cards	❐ Laser pointer
❐ Clear tape	❐ Masking tape
❐ Correction fluid	❐ Whiteboard markers
❐ Blank paper / heavier stock paper	❐ Flipchart markers
	❐ Paper
❐ Duct tape or gaff tape for extension cord safety	❐ Paper clips
	❐ Pencil sharpener
❐ Erasers	❐ Pens and sharpened
❐ Extension cord and power strip	pencils
	❐ Post-it notes
❐ Jump drive or blank CD/ DVDs	❐ Projector bulbs
	❐ Rubber bands
❐ Grease pencil or transparency markers	❐ Scissors
	❐ Stapler & staple remover
❐ Highlighter	❐ Tape measure and ruler
❐ Hole punch	❐ Transparencies

7. After you have settled into the presentation location, check to make sure any audiovisual equipment you plan to use is in working order and that you are familiar with its operation.

8. Do a quick check of the room. Note where the light switches are located and how they function. Check to make sure that your audience is able to see you and any audiovisuals you plan to use. Check for loose cords or any other possible hazards to your audience and you. Make sure your microphone works and if possible do a sound check by asking someone to stand at the back of the room to ensure you will be heard by everyone in the audience.

9. Look at yourself in a mirror.

10. If possible, greet your audience members as they arrive. This little gesture boosts your credibility and helps your audience have a better impression of you.

11. Run through the last-minute checklists to ensure you have covered all bases.

STEP **10**

12. Take a deep breath, run through your positive visualization or the first 90 minutes of the presentation. Use your positive self-talk to say "I'm prepared and I'm going to knock this presentation out of the ballpark!"

Resolving Logistical Issues

Although there are many logistical-issue scenarios and challenges with audience members that can't be enumerated in the space available in this book, this section focuses on some of the most common issues and snafus that may occur so that you'll be prepared with ideas of how to appropriately handle the situation and look like a seasoned professional doing so.

Wrong Room Setup

One gotcha—arriving at the presentation site only to find that the room has not been set up as you requested—is easily solved if you arrive early enough to make the adjustments or get site staff to help with this process. No matter how much you planned, communicated the setup, double-checked that the site understood the correct setup—this will happen to you at some point during your presentation career.

First, assess the situation and determine if the audience will be able to see and hear you. If you can work with the setup, then don't sweat it and make a few adjustments as needed.

If the setup is a big issue, contact the appropriate person at the presentation site and explain what you need. Don't get upset or place blame. You're trying to enlist allies to help you solve the situation quickly—so you don't want to alienate anyone. Explain exactly what you need for the room setup to work.

In any case, do not settle for a room setup that prevents you from successfully delivering your presentation or is a barrier to the audience being able to easily see and hear your message.

External Noise

Imagine that you are in the middle of your presentation and you hear the ratta-tat-tat of a drill in the wall or the whirr of a leaf blower outside the window. The fact of the matter is that neither you nor your audience should have to endure this noise and distraction. If closing the door does not resolve the situation, ask the site authority if another room is available or if the noise could be stopped until the end of your presentation. As the speaker, you are responsible for addressing these situations quickly when they come up. Do not just throw up your hands and apologize to your audience.

Large Room with Few Participants

If only a few people show up for your speech, don't take it personally. Someone probably dropped the ball when it came to marketing and advertising the presentation. Try to coax the participants to the front of the room with something like, "You look a little lonely out there, would you mind sitting a little closer to the front? I promise not to embarrass you if you sit in the front row." Humor can build rapport with the audience and make them feel comfortable and accepting of what you have to say. Taking a schoolmarmish approach by asking the attendees to "move to the head of the class" will not help you to deal with this situation.

Audiovisual Equipment

You've tested the audiovisual equipment and all is going well. In the middle of your presentation, you hear a "pop," and the projector goes dark. If needed, take a 5- or 10-minute break and contact the audiovisual expert to see how quickly the situation can be resolved. If the equipment can't be fixed in the time you have for

STEP **10**

your presentation—then follow your contingency plan to use a flipchart or rely on handouts.

Many speakers bring flipcharts and set them up—even though they might not need them. Often, they write in pencil in the corners of the flipcharts so that they have cheat-sheet notes that are "invisible" to the audience just in case something goes wrong.

If you provided handouts, for example, copies of the slides you are going to discuss—then direct everyone's attention to the appropriate pages detailing the key points, facts, illustrations, or other information as you smoothly continue with the presentation.

As a best practice, keep your cool and use humor to explain the situation. Most audiences will understand if you handle the situation appropriately.

Wrong Flipchart Holder/Easel

Just when you thought you had all of the logistics covered—confirming that a flipchart easel was going to be provided for your masterfully legible and intriguing flipcharts—you discover that not all flipchart paper and easels go together. If you find that the flipchart paper holes are positioned differently from the easel—or if the easel only has a flimsy bar at the bottom that won't hold your charts in place, try to jury-rig a solution. For example, can you punch the holes in a different location on your pages, or use a coat hanger to come up with a solution? As a worst-case scenario, if you have masking tape in your contingency kit, you can tape the individual flipchart pages to the stand.

Dropping Notes or Other Materials

So what happens when you drop your notes, transparencies, or other materials? Gracefully swoop down to pick up the materials and perhaps say to the audience something like, "I always wondered what would happen if I dropped all of my _____ . . . and now I know. If you'll bear with me a moment, I'll put these back in order and we'll be ready to go."

Resolving Audience Issues

Disruptive Audience Members

In most instances, realize that most of the audience is on your side and would like for the disruption to stop. On the other hand, the audience is clearly waiting to see how you handle the situation. If you get angry, you have lost control—and your credibility. The most unobtrusive way of handling inappropriate behavior is to look at the misbehaving audience member for 3 to 5 seconds as if to say, "stop it!" If this approach doesn't work, ask if the participant has a specific question or comment. Third-grade teachers handle disruptive children this way, and it usually works for adults, too. If the disruption continues, take a break and speak to the disruptive individual directly and offline.

Eager Beaver Questioner

Questions are good because they show interest if not always agreement. There are times, however, when one participant may try to dominate the session by asking repeated questions. When dealing with incessant question-askers, acknowledge his or her interest but explain that due to the time constraints of the session you do not have time to answer all questions, and then move on. You could also explain that you will field all questions at the end of the session or that you are willing to even stay after the session to answer all questions in case time does not permit during the allotted time for the presentation.

Dead Silence

What if no one has any questions? It can definitely be an awkward moment if you invite questions and then the room becomes so quiet that you could hear a pin drop. This situation is especially challenging if you have set aside a specific amount of time for Q&A at the end of the session.

STEP 10

The reason for the silence could be two-fold. For example, perhaps the audience members are just trying to process all of the information and are thinking it through to develop some questions. If this is the case, then perhaps a short break will give them time to formulate some questions.

Or, if the audience truly does not have any questions—there is no reason that you couldn't pose questions to them about the subject. You'll usually get a response or two that leads into questions or a healthy discussion that is of value to the audience members and helps to fill your allotted Q&A time.

When a Participant Strongly Disagrees with Your Point of View

If an audience member strongly disagrees with your point of view, consider these tips as a way to help diffuse the situation:

- Remember that everyone is entitled to an opinion, so don't take it personally and feel hurt or angry.
- If you feel that the disagreement is becoming personal, direct the conversation back to the subject of the presentation. Remember, the presentation is about your subject, not about you. Don't fall into the trap of trying to defend yourself—this is a no-win situation and usually results in a loss of credibility for the speaker.
- Acknowledge the other point of view and be respectful of audience-member opinions. Don't agree to something that you disagree with. Instead, use your facilitation techniques to solicit opinions from other audience members and to draw them into the conversation.
- Ultimately, as the presenter, you need to control the presentation. This means having to use your authority at times to politely direct the conversation elsewhere and move on.

Waiting for Late Arrivals

Another common dilemma that every presenter will experience at some point is a half-empty room and whether or not to wait a few more minutes for latecomers or just to dive in to the content for the participants who arrived on time. If this situation isn't handled appropriately this is surely an are that can damage your credibility.

When making the decision of whether to wait or forge ahead, consult the sponsor on whether to begin or not. Let the audience know that you are going to wait another 5 or 10 minutes and that you will them move ahead and do your best to get any latecomers caught up on what you are presenting. Whatever your decision is in this situation, be sure to stick to what you've promised.

Your hard work has paid off and you have successfully completed your presentation! Take a moment and reflect on your performance. Use Worksheet 10.1 to assess your planning and delivery accurately, so you can use this experience to enhance your next presentation.

STEP **10**

WORKSHEET 10.1

Presentation Planning & Improvement Worksheet

Even though you have worked your way through the process of perhaps creating and delivering a presentation, the process doesn't end there. Successful presenters make time after every presentation to reflect on the successes of the session and document ideas for improving future speeches. Use this checklist to help you work on presentation planning, delivery, and facilitation skills. Check "Yes" or "No" answers for each item. Note that any "no" answers may indicate weaknesses in your process. Record possible solutions and ways to improve your presentation in the comments section.

PLANNING:	Yes	No	Comments
Audience Profile			
1. Determined the number of participants and planned to accommodate that number.			
2. Took into account participants' reasons for attending the presentation.			
3. Reviewed audience background and experience and considered this information in planning of presentation.			
Topic Research			
1. Established presentation goals and objectives.			
2. Reviewed presentation content for accuracy, relevance, and clarity.			
3. Allotted sufficient time for the presentation.			
Presentation Site Planning			
1. Meeting room was comfortable. Temperature, lighting were adequate.			
2. Tables and chairs were arranged to suit participants' needs.			
3. All audiovisual equipment was checked and in working order.			
4. Writing boards and flipcharts were available.			
5. Break-out rooms, meals, or refreshments were available as scheduled.			

DELIVERY :	Yes	No	Comments
Verbal and Nonverbal Communication			
1. Dressed appropriately.			
2. Had satisfactory voice projection, pitch, tone, and volume.			
3. Introduced presentation effectively; captured audience attention and interest during the rest of the presentation.			
4. Maintained eye contact.			
5. Used body language to express confidence and enhance presentation.			
6. Used facial expressions effectively; engaged participants in discussion and invited them to contribute ideas and comments.			
7. Moved around the room and gestured to emphasize and reinforce key points of the presentation.			
8. Showed sincere enthusiasm.			
9. Used gestures that were not distracting.			
10. Communicated on a personal level.			
11. Emphasized key points and used relevant examples.			
12. Used effective visual aids.			
13. Made logical, smooth transitions between key and supporting points.			
14. Provided a comprehensive, easy-to-follow summary.			

Questioning and Reinforcement

1. Asked key questions.
2. Directed questions to the entire group.
3. Addressed individuals by name.
4. Walked toward individuals when addressing them.
5. Offered participants praise and reinforcement.
6. Asked questions on a variety of levels.
7. Repeated or paraphrased participants' questions or responses for the benefit of the group.

Humor

1. Used humor effectively. Jokes and stories illustrated key points.
2. Used humor that was acceptable to the group and never offensive.
3. Laughed with individuals, never at them.
4. Used topic-related cartoons, drawings, and illustrations to reinforce the key or supporting points of the presentation.

STEP
10

STEP 10

STEP 10

BIBLIOGRAPHY

Bedrosian, M. (reprinted 1995). "How to Make a Large Group Presentation." *Infoline* No. 259102. Alexandria, VA: ASTD Press.

Biech, E., M. Danahy, and B. Drake. (reprinted 1993). "Diagnostic Tools for Quality Control." *Infoline* No.259109. Alexandria, VA: ASTD Press.

Callahan, M., and C. Russo, eds. (1999) "10 Great Games and How to Use Them." *Infoline* No. 258411. Alexandria, VA: ASTD Press.

Cassidy, Michael. (1999). "Group Decision Making." *Infoline* No. 259906. Alexandria, VA: ASTD Press.

Darraugh, Barbara. (reprinted 2000). "How to Facilitate." *Infoline* No. 259406. Alexandria, VA: ASTD Press.

———. (reprinted 1997). "Group Process Tools." *Infoline* No. 259407. Alexandria, VA: ASTD Press.

Eline, L. (revised 1997). "How to Prepare and Use Effective Visual Aids." *Infoline* No. 258410. Alexandria, VA: ASTD Press.

Estep, T. (2005). "Meetings that Work!" *Infoline* No. 250505. Alexandria, VA: ASTD Press.

Finkel, C., and A. Finkel. (revised 2000). "Facilities Planning." *Infoline* No. 258504. Alexandria, VA: ASTD Press.

Jacobson, S. (1994). "Neurolinguistic Programming." *Infoline* No. 259404. Alexandria, VA: ASTD Press.

Kirkpatrick, Donald. (2006). *How to Conduct Productive Meetings.* Alexandria, VA: ASTD Press.

Kirrane, D. (1988). "Be a Better Speaker." *Infoline* No. 258802. Alexandria, VA: ASTD Press.

McCain, D., and D. Tobey. (2004). *Facilitation Basics*. Alexandria, VA: ASTD Press.

Merriam-Webster's Collegiate Dictionary (11th ed.). (2003). Springfield, MA: Merriam-Webster.

Piskurich, G. (2002). *HPI Essentials*. Alexandria, VA: ASTD Press.

Prezioso, R. (revised 1999). "Icebreakers." *Infoline* No. 258911. Alexandria, VA: ASTD Press.

Rosania, R.J. (2003). *Presentation Basics*. Alexandria, VA: ASTD Press.

Russo, C.S. (2000). "Storytelling." *Infoline* No. 250006. Alexandria, VA: ASTD Press.

Spruell, G. (revised 1997). "More Productive Meetings." *Infoline* No. 258710. Alexandria, VA: ASTD Press.

Wircenski, J., and R. Sullivan. (1986). "Make Every Presentation a Winner." *Infoline* No. 258606. Alexandria, VA: ASTD Press.

I N D E X

Training sessions, 20
Transitions, 34–35, 38, 145
Type of presentation, determination
  of, 19-21
Typefaces, 82

U
U-shape configuration, 97–99
Unanticipated events, 169–80
Unconscious body language, 117
Understandability, as quality of
  effective presentation, 39

V
Value, as quality of effective
  presentation, 38
Various opinions, accepting, 125
Venue, 95–110. *See also* Physical
  environment
Verbal communication skills,
  111–15
Video camera, 149
Videotapes, 63–64
  advantages of, 64
  when not to use, 64
Vision, use of, 41
Visual aids, 45–70
  assessment of, 67–68
  benefits of, 46
  color, use of, 50
  design of, consistency, 48–49
  DVDs, 63–64
    advantages of, 64
    when not to use, 64
  early preparation of, 49
  flipcharts, 51–55
    advantages of, 53–54
    when not to use, 54–55
  graphic visuals
    analogies, 83–84
    elaborate, 82
    graphs, 84
    guidelines for, 81
    lack of clutter, 82
    metaphors, 83
    quotations, 83

serif, selection of, 82
slides, displaying text, 82
tables, 84
typefaces, 82
white space, use of, 82
guidelines for, 48–49
handouts, 64–65
number of visuals, 48
one point per visual, 48
orientation of, 49
overhead transparencies, 55–59
  advantages of, 57
  creating, 58–59
  when not to use, 57–58
PowerPoint, 59–62
  presentation software, 59–62
  advantages of, 59–60
  when not to use, 61
props, 66
redundant information, avoiding,
  48
repetition of information, 49
selection of, 46–47
slides, 62–63
  advantages of, 62
  when not to use, 62–63
steps for adding, 49–50
symbolism, use of, 66
talking to audience, 49
text, 82–84
  positioning of, 49
  use of, 80–84
touch, turn, talk method, 51–52
videotapes, 63–64
  advantages of, 64
  when not to use, 64
Visualization techniques, 154

W
Warm-up exercises, 72, 155–56
White space, use of, 82
Wireless microphones, 105
Wobbly knees, 160
Wrong flipchart holder/easel, 174
Wrong room setup, 172–73

THE ASTD MISSION:

Through exceptional learning and performance, we create a world that works better.

The American Society for Training & Development provides world-class professional development opportunities, content, networking, and resources for workplace learning and performance professionals.

Dedicated to helping members increase their relevance, enhance their skills, and align learning to business results, ASTD sets the standard for best practices within the profession.

The society is recognized for shaping global discussions on workforce development and providing the tools to demonstrate the impact of learning on the organizational bottom line. ASTD represents the profession's interests to corporate executives, policy makers, academic leaders, small business owners, and consultants through world-class content, convening opportunities, professional development, and awards and recognition.

Resources
- *T+D (Training + Development)* Magazine
- ASTD Press
- Industry Newsletters
- Research and Benchmarking
- Representation to Policy Makers

Networking
- Local Chapters
- Online Communities
- ASTD Connect
- Benchmarking Forum
- Learning Executives Network

Professional Development
- Certificate Programs
- Conferences and Workshops
- Online Learning
- CPLP™ Certification Through the ASTD Certification Institute
- Career Center and Job Bank

Awards and Best Practices
- ASTD BEST Awards
- Excellence in Practice Awards
- E-Learning Courseware Certification (ECC) Through the ASTD Certification Institute

Learn more about ASTD at www.astd.org.
1.800.628.2783 (U.S.) or 1.703.683.8100
customercare@astd.org

ALSO IN THIS SERIES

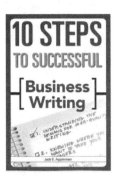

10 Steps to Successful Business Writing

Jack E. Appleman

Poor writing and communication skills directly impact organizational productivity. From understanding the importance of communicating clearly to the absolute necessity of editing and revising your work, the advice offered by veteran writing expert Jack Appleman is practical and concise. He offers simple strategies in digestible bits anyone can implement, including dozens of relevant examples to point your way to success as new skills are developed and you increase your influence and credibility with each well-honed, clear email, memo, or letter you write.

Product order code: **110716**
ISBN: **978-1-56286-481-1**
List price: **$19.95**

10 Steps to Be a Successful Manager

Lisa Haneberg

Here's a primer for on-the-job success as a manager, regardless of your years of experience. A simple, straightforward 10-step model aligns your management practices for improved results and communications that help you build a great work team and ensure that your staff clearly understands performance success and expectations. Tools are provided to help you clarify what's expected of you and how to determine if you are still on track. Worksheets are included for everything from weekly planning to measurement tools.

Product order code: **110710**
ISBN: **978-1-56286-475-0**
List price: **$19.95**

And turn the page for more great choices!

10 Steps to Be a Successful Manager: Facilitator's Guide

Lisa Haneberg

Get off the "no-progress treadmill" and make the most of the *10 Steps to Be a Successful Manager* by putting them into action now. This companion facilitator's guide offers trainers, coaches, and other training professionals the structure they need to create great management training that gets results. Rather than a traditional workbook with play-by-play facilitation instructions, you'll discover a roadmap for manager training that can be effective at the team, group, division, or even individual level. You will also find a variety of ready-to-use tables, tools, and worksheets to help create meaningful training experiences. The help you need to be a positive catalyst in your organization is at your fingertips.

Product order code: **110711**
ISBN: **978-1-56286-476-7**
List price: **$29.95**

10 Steps to Successful Project Management

Lou Russell

Project management is a key business skill no matter your position in the organization. *10 Steps to Successful Project Management* offers you a crash course on how to ensure that your next project is delivered on time. You will learn how to distinguish between a project and a task, build a convincing business case, define the scope of the project, weigh the risks and constraints, collaborate, create a project blueprint, determine the tangible and intangible components of a project, and review lessons learned. This is a critical reference for anyone wishing to improve their project management skills.

Product order code: **110705**
ISBN: **978-1-56286-463-7**
List price: **$19.95**

And turn the page for more great choices!

10 Steps to Successful Strategic Planning

Susan Barksdale and Teri Lund

A strategic plan is central to a company's ability to make critical business decisions and develop a mission and vision that will inspire and excite employees, customers, partners, and shareholders. *10 Steps to Successful Strategic Planning* offers a simple process to help you get your organization on the path to planned success. Loaded with worksheets, exercises, tips, tools, checklists, and other easy-to-use learning aids, this book walks you through the process from beginning to end.

Product order code: **110613**
ISBN: **978-1-56286-457-6**
List price: **$19.95**